The Stone

Mosaic

by
Oceola Winslow

The Stone Mosaic
©2018 by Oceola Winslow. All rights reserved.

Published by Proper Publishing LLC.
Book and cover design ©2018
By Proper Publishing LLC.
www.properpublishing.info
theproperpublisher@yahoo.com
If you're going to publish, do it properly.

Dedicated

To the
Unseen One
Designer of Life
Source of Comfort
Sustainer of Things Worthy
Provider of Strength for Daily Tasks

בָּרוּךְ אַתָּה יְיָ אֱלֹהֵינוּ מֶלֶךְ הָעוֹלָם
Blessed are you, Lord, our God, sovereign of the
universe.

Note:
Consider it worth your time to reference the following:
✧Verse 36 of chapter 11 in Romans
✧First Corinthians chapter 8, verse 6
✧The fourth chapter of Revelation, eleventh verse.
Ponder the enormity of this mystery. In the process of living
more than eighty five years, the author has discovered
concepts recorded in the Bible to be trustworthy stepping
stones and pillars of rock to hold fast.

Introduction

Sweeping away ashes of temporary emotions often reveals stones of value.

The author has written a collection of actual personal experiences. Time provided a mental broom that was used to find *truth*, sometimes hidden under deep layers of memory.

If any of these shared stories can encourage just one person, then the effort is truly worthwhile.

Index

Early Childhood Memories
"have lasting impact"

"I can swim, Mommy. I can swim, Mommy."
I used louder voice this time in case she for
some reason did not hear me. At the same time I also
pushed with all my strength against her arms that
would not release me to the water. Mother held me
firmly. This time I begged her, "I can swim, Mommy."
Why didn't she believe me?

Perhaps it was because I was just a toddler. As
my parent she knew I had not been given swim
lessons. She was determined to protect her only child.
But I was speaking truth and she would not listen.
Finally, I gave up and simply looked around at the
other people in the huge community swimming pool
at Redd's Beach. Mom had no idea how I felt.
Grandma Lansdale, my mother's mom was with us.
She did not speak one word. I wanted to kick and
scream. I forced the tears to remain in my eyes. You
see, my Mother would not allow me to cry. If at times
I would begin to sob she would warn me that I was
setting myself up to receive something to really cry
about from her. Being an only child not planned or
warmly welcomed at birth I had no frame of reference.
There were no siblings to share the stringent set of
standards that a good little girl should maintain.

I kept my thoughts to myself the rest of the
afternoon at the gathering place of country folk
enjoying a glimpse of rollicking on a sandy beach at
ocean side. We were landlocked in the foothills of
Western Pennsylvania.

Silence has its own reward. You hear things. Others do not realize the extent of your awareness. Mother and Grandma changed into the usual farmer style dresses of cotton print. They packed up the stuff they brought and put me in the middle of the stuff on the back seat of the car. I listened to Mother as she drove along the road. Can you imagine Oceola thought she could swim? Grandma simply did not respond. Did she know? Did she know I could really swim?

I remember that day at Redd's beach with vivid frustration. I really do believe that intuitively I knew how to swim. Ever watch a supervised baby paddle its arms and legs when placed in the water? How do adults know the things their offspring can truly do? Do parents really understand what even infants already know? I can even remember the wall paper on the wall in the rented room in which I was born. I can see people peering down at me saying "isn't she tiny?" Thankfully not all the wisdom that arrived with my tiny person was destroyed by society's beliefs and customs. Fortunately, folks along the way, including my well-meaning Mommy, encouraged my efforts to build one block upon another forming the structure of the 86 year old woman who is writing this memoir.

Another vivid memory for me is listening to my Father speak to my Mother in the car on the way home from a meeting at a little country church. I was sitting between them. They both thought I could not understand the conversation. "Can you imagine Oceola put her hand up for prayer?" This time it was Mother who did not speak a word. She was quiet the rest of the way home. I had listened intently to the words of the preacher as he gave his sermon. At the conclusion he asked those in the church to raise their hands if they wanted him to pray for them. No, I did not grasp the entire concept. What I knew for certain was that I felt something within me that was mysterious. When I raised my hand Dad leaned over and firmly told me to put my hand down. Feeling ashamed I obeyed. Thankfully, that well intended request did not snuff out my awareness of something beyond, something greater than my place with my parents.

A few years later, in the second grade, I became a good reader. The preacher gave me a book. The book declared that "Santa Claus" was a well-meaning myth that parents used, to provide excitement and gifts for children at Christmas time. Mom and Dad had adroitly dodged my observation that the beard was a fake on the Santa Claus at the store. Armed with the truth discovered in the book from Reverend Bishop I confronted my parents with these words of total dismay, "You lied to me. There is no Santa Claus. How can I believe anything you have told me?"

My parents were embarrassed. They tried valiantly to placate me. For the rest of my life I have hesitated to trust words spoken by other people. Like a coin, I have discovered there are two sides that do not match. It is a good thing to consider both.

Another early childhood memory centers on a postcard. It fascinated me. It had ten colorful squares on it with pictures. Each picture symbolized one of the Ten Commandments. I was six years old. The teacher in my Sunday school class at the Methodist Church had given each child in her class the same post card. Some took the card and gave it to their parents. Others left their cards lying in church. The card was precious to me. I did not know the reason. I asked the class teacher to explain why each picture was different yet the same size. Thoughts kept running through my mind about each square. That little card was part of my memoirs when I left home to begin living alone and earning money to support myself.

The introduction of the Ten Commandments to a young child had effects beyond the moment. I observed that society functions well when these are practiced. I learned as I matured into adulthood that the true value could be divided into two questions. How do I happen to live on this tiny planet in this vast universe? Why and for what purpose? Once again I am reminded of the coin with two different sides.

* * * * *

Early memories are like typeset on printing presses in our personhood, they leave marks. Experiences of a whole life time meld together. Coupled with our inherited genes we each become truly unique. This gives me joy. It also gives me sadness for others and for myself with memories that present challenges. This I know for certain; I can sprinkle kindness each day; I can truly listen to sounds of the moment; I can simply be available to give lasting gifts of love when the time is appropriate.

Facets of Discipline
"learning from mistakes"

Being an only child can be both good and bad. You are forced to face authority alone, entertain yourself, and miss the early learning of interaction with peers. Being the focus of attention can highlight your failures.

Martha Sue was the only playmate I knew before starting school. She lived in a new house her father built across the creek. You could look out our kitchen window and see Martha's home. My parents were friendly with their new neighbors. Mother and Mrs.Yankowski would have long talks. Dad and Joe Yankowski liked to do men chats about work, gardens, and the challenges of working with cars, tools, etc. They were not aware that I was listening intently to their conversations.

Martha had one brother when the family moved into the house. Soon Mrs.Yankowski developed a huge belly and in my rather innocent childhood thoughts knew that another child would soon be on the scene. Timmy arrived and immediately became the center of his parent's attention. Joe Yankowski however, managed to give some time to his other son, Raymond. He was proud of his boys. Dad was envious. Neither man had time for the little girls who were part of the family.

Martha was about two years younger than I but we found great delight in playing in the woods, exploring trees, all kinds of plants, stones in the clear water of the creek, climbing the wood rail fences. We shared a special love for a favorite toy that my parents built. It was a huge swing anchored between two giant poplar trees. Dad had brought home a railroad timber. He was joined by four of his buddies at work. One man had a forklift. As a team the men, using heavy log chains had managed to get the timber up to the strong branches of each tree. The whole effort took the entire day. The swing's rope was the type used by riverboats on the Monongahela River. Dad also fashioned a large wooden seat held securely by running the rope through large holes on either side of the wooden seat. Kids were dwarfed by the swing. It was the perfect size for adults. Mom's Sunday School Class of High School girls loved the swing. I would sit on the front steps and watch them.

Martha and I did not use the adult size swing as it was intended. We developed imaginative ways of twisting the rope then jumping on and letting the laws of physics whip us round and round as we laughed and squealed. We would also jump on either side of the swing with our feet, holding the rope fervently with our hands while we used our little bodies to gain momentum in the sideway motion until we almost hit each of the trees holding up the swing.

Our friendship lasted until the fall that Mother drove me to First Grade class in one of the river towns in Pennsylvania. This was a sacrifice for her. Tuition was charged because I did not live in the jurisdiction of the river town. Mom wanted me to receive a better education than a one room school could offer. Having developed a method of entertaining myself, it was difficult to transition to recess time at school. I did not know the other children. They mostly treated me as the odd girl from the country. Mom insisted that I wear dresses above my knees and in addition I had to wear long brown cotton stockings held up by a garment with "supporters" that was similar to a jacket. In classroom pictures, I would stand out as an odd child. I hated it. But Mom would not even discuss the matter. She understood that she was the Mother and I was the daughter. Children did as they were told.

Today I appreciate Mom's discipline and teaching. She gave me a good foundation for living life. When I was an adult Mother would say to me, "Georgie, no parent is perfect. We only do the best we know how." Of course, she was right. However, I do recall one occasion of discipline that leaves me with mixed emotions. I had managed to make friends with two sisters in Roscoe, one with bright red hair named Sharma Jean. The other sister had blonde hair. Her parents named her Iris Ann. They were very well dressed and had lovely dolls, dollhouses, doll clothes. The array made me astonished. Sharma Jean, the red head was in the same grade with me. Iris Ann was one year behind. We would walk from school to the sister's home where Mom would pick me up. It worked out well for I could play with the pretty dolls and feel part of a family while waiting. Mom was often late in arriving. She would be out hunting for a farm to buy and misjudge the time needed get to the river town school.

One weekend, the sisters' parents, thought it would be a good idea for the girls to experience a bit of farm life and see the animals. Sharma Jean and Iris Ann were also eager to try out the swing that I often talked about. The girls spent the day with me. Martha

Sue, my old playmate joined us uninvited. I resented that. From this point in my life's journey I believe I was ashamed of Martha. She acted and represented the country bumpkin image that was truly a part of our lives. I had tasted the outside world and liked what I saw. The four of us did not get along that day. We said ugly things to each other. Martha was obviously hurt and felt rejected.

The next day Martha arrived at our door. She wanted to speak to Mrs.Winslow. I was surprised for I had already forgotten the day before. When Mom came to the front door, Martha looked up at her and said in front of me, "Oceola fought with me yesterday." Mom turned to me and asked if that statement had truth. I said yes. Without another word Mother went into the kitchen, pulled out her wooden paddle, turned me over her lap and gave me many good wallops. "No daughter of mine, fights." She shouted. Martha had a smug look on her face. My humiliation was delicious revenge.

The result of that discipline developed within me several attributes. I made a vow to NEVER tell another person with power about something that happened to me. I also developed a tough stance with bullies. Since my conduct with Martha had been one of a bully, I discovered that bullies only do what they think they can get away with. I quickly put that knowledge to work on a walk from school to the sisters' home. The three of us were confronted by some tough talking boys. Sharma Jean and Iris Ann quickly screamed and ran. I stood my ground. I put my hands on my hips and stared at them with a vicious scowl. "Who do you think you are? Leave or face the consequences." My voice was low and menacing. It came from somewhere very deep inside of me. Strangely, the boys who outnumbered me, and who were all stronger than I backed away. Perhaps they had never seen rage of the sort that emanated from me. But I was given a sense of courage in that moment. The same courage has served me well through my nearly 86 years. I am grateful.

As for the humiliation, I truly believe there is a better way to solve disputes than being a tattletale. If I were Oceola's mother, would I have paddled her in front of her accuser? Maybe! Perhaps Mom was having a bad day. Perhaps she was embarrassed that her neighbors, the Yankowski Family would think despairingly of the Winslow Family. In my adult years disagreements between Mother and I were handled by frank exchanges of words. Each expressed their point of view. We did not always agree but still cherished each other.

Martha Sue began school that year. Her parents sent her to the one room school in the rural community. She married and had seven children. We saw each other many years later when David and I took a memory trip back to Pennsylvania. Martha was living with her widowed mother. Martha's husband left his family for another woman. One of Martha's brothers had died of a heart attack. In spite of these challenges my first playmate had developed a childlike trust in God. We spent a wonderful hour together, parting with tears and hugs.

*****

In the aging process things that loomed as major, have taken on a minor roll. I learned not to BE a bully but simply rely on inner strength when faced BY a bully. I learned to accept the consequences of doing things that are unkind. I also learned that trying to impress others is a waste of precious time.

Educating A Country Girl-Part One
"a trilogy"

Adelia and Elizabeth Lansdale, two elderly spinsters, were the proprietors of an upscale room and board in the swank Shady Side Neighborhood of Pittsburgh, Pennsylvania. They also conducted what we would call today a refinement camp for country bumpkins. In the summer during school recess Mother would send me to this camp for a week.

The unstated but understood purpose of the week was designed to teach young girls the ways of proper conduct in society. There was no doubt about the focus. There was no shortage of instructors. I was the only camper and I had two instructors, Adelia and Elizabeth. They were well organized. My days were carefully planned. Being the only camper did not bother me too much since I already knew the privilege and burden of being an only child.

Adelia and Elizabeth Lansdale were two sisters of my Grandfather Preston Lansdale. They had managed to escape the simple and rugged ways of a farm in the mountains of Western Pennsylvania.

Adelia wanted no part of rural life so she hired out as a servant to a wealthy German couple living in nearby Uniontown. The Rosenbaums owned and operated a prestigious department store offering the finest selections of merchandise southwest of Pittsburgh. It was from this couple that Adelia learned the art of setting a proper table. She observed the protocol of which fork, spoon, or knife should be used for each course. Adelia also learned how a society household functioned. She was twenty-four, tall and slender, and made a fine appearance in her uniform. In early years on the farm Adelia had developed the frugal life style. Working as a servant she was able to accumulate a sum of money.

Another sister, Julia, also left the farm. She went directly to Pittsburgh and hired out as a seamstress. She, too, made use of her knowledge of a simple life and stashed cash as she worked. Adelia learned about the opportunities in the big city from Julia so she joined her sister. The two girls urged another sister, Elizabeth, to leave the drudgery of farm life. Together the three unmarried sisters located a room and board facility in an upscale neighborhood in Pittsburgh's Shady Side. The facility was a three story brick home located just two blocks from the prestigious Fifth Avenue. Fifth Avenue was lined with huge splendid mansions. It also had electric trolley cars running every half hour into Pittsburgh's downtown shopping area. Also accessible were cultural buildings including The University of Pittsburgh, and The Pittsburgh Symphony and Opera House. Trolley cars also serviced the thriving East Liberty Suburb and its neighbor Highland Park in which the Zoo was located.

Julia Lansdale was the adventurous one of the three sisters. Shortly after Adelia and Elizabeth moved to the city Julia took a course in business skills and found a position in Washington, D.C. We are not sure if any of the two remaining sisters worked for the owners of the room and board establishment. We do know that when their father, Adam Lansdale died, their mother, Matilda Lansdale, moved to Pittsburgh to live with her daughters. It was the same year, 1921, that the trio purchased the building on Ivy Street. It continued operations as a room and board. The deed indicates that the building was sold to the sisters for one dollar plus other consideration. This may indicate that the Lansdale sisters had indeed been involved in the operation of the room and board establishment before the purchase.

The house on Ivy Street had many fine features. There was an elegant parlor to the right of the entry replete with an elegant fireplace. The reception hall was grand with a winding staircase, and a stained glass window at the first landing. The ceiling was two stories high. Leading off the impressive hall was an equally impressive dining room. It filled the entire width of the house and fully one third of the length. During my visits I learned that every evening over forty people dined there in two sittings. The dining room had two large tables covered in fine white linen, a beautiful fireplace, a huge sideboard housing fine china and sterling silver. There was a lovely cabinet with glass doors. It housed an exquisite collection of "salt sellers". This was a true delight to me. I carefully looked at each piece but was not allowed to touch them.

The sisters, Adelia and Elizabeth, had created a routine that worked extremely well. Adelia was an excellent cook. Even as a very finicky eater, I savored every bite of food that she prepared. Early in the day after the live in boarders were served breakfast and were out working in their various vocations, the sisters would begin preparing the evening meal. Elizabeth did mostly the support work such as chopping, washing vegetables, peeling fruit for pies etc. Adelia was in charge of the finesse of adding spices and doing the final cooking. We would find their work very challenging today. They used a monster sized black iron stove which was coal fired. How they ever managed to avoid burning the lovely cakes and pies produced is truly a mystery. At serving time Adelia would place the portions on each plate and Elizabeth would adroitly balance four plates on her arms and hands and carry them to the dining room. She always carefully served from the proper side while softly stating each diner's name as she placed the plate of luscious looking food in front of them. My job was to keep out of the way. Aunt Elizabeth would say, "Stand back now, Child. Keep away from the swing door." It was understood that I was not to be seen by the paying guests. The Lansdale sisters had a strong reputation for serving consistently fine food at reasonable prices. They always had a waiting list of hopeful diners who lived in apartments and rooms around the Shadyside community. The regular diners included attorneys, department store buyers, and professors from the nearby University of Pittsburgh and Carnegie Mellon University.

Our country was at war during many of my summer camp experiences with the "girls" as we call them. As part of my schedule, I would walk with Adelia the three blocks to do her regular grocery shopping. She carried a separate bag with blue and red ration tokens. All the regular diners at the Lansdale Sister's Room and Board would give Elizabeth their portion of tokens. They were pooled and placed in Adelia's special bag for shopping.

The local butcher knew Adelia's preferences for cuts of meat. I recall that he would set aside portions to present to her when we entered his shop. Adelia preferred the less popular cuts of meat and knew how to make them so tender, that when served that you could avoid using your knife to break the meat into bite-sized pieces. After the butcher Auntie and I would visit the general store for staples like coffee, tea, sugar and flour. Adelia created and baked all of the bread, pies, cakes and luscious donuts served at the Lansdale Room and Board.

The final stop on our shopping errand was the fresh vegetable and fruit stand. Adelia would fuss and fume while looking for the best selections. These would make up each menu since the frugality she had learned on the farm was put to use wisely. The girls made a nifty profit on each meal served. Elizabeth was the bookkeeper. She collected on a weekly basis the cost of the meals in advance. Rarely did a diner miss a meal.

The Lansdale girls were not stingy. At least six male students from Carnegie Mellon and the University of Pittsburgh were hired to help serve and wash dishes after the meals. The boys were given free meals and a modest wage. This enabled them to financially complete their degrees. All the students became devotees of the Lansdale sisters. After graduation they would often visit. The sisters were invited to their weddings. Pictures were sent of the children each Christmas.

My camp training was not all drudgery. The girls would make time to take me to the "motion picture shows" also located just three blocks from their house. I remember seeing Ginger Rogers and Fred Astaire in several pictures. Also remember the movie called "I'll be Seeing You" made famous by the theme song with the same title. It is not surprising that the girls enjoyed romance and comedy since most of their days were spent doing hard work.

Aunt Elizabeth assigned me a white cloth and guided my efforts as I dusted the many spindles in the long winding stairway in the reception hall. She would briskly run the mechanical sweeper over the lovely rugs on the first floor. Both Elizabeth and Adelia scrubbed the white table linens, towels, and bed sheets by hand in the basement. The laundered items were hung to dry in the back yard fenced in for privacy. The sisters would take turns ironing the laundry. The linens were always perfectly white. They used a blue liquid called "Bluing" to maintain the pristine condition. The tablecloths received a slight rinse of starch for crispness.

The girls selected their own rooms in strategic places in the house. Aunt Elizabeth's room was on the second floor in a former linen closet. The room was just large enough to house a single bed and very small dresser. The larger rooms were rented. Elizabeth had excellent hearing and could respond with astounding speed to any sound that indicated something was amiss. Aunt Adelia's room was on the third floor at the back of the large brick house. It was the servant's quarters. A separate narrow spiraling stair led from just outside her room directly to the kitchen.

I was assigned to sleep with Aunt Adelia during my camp experience. It was fascinating to watch the elderly lady (about 68-years-old) comb her gray hair over a hair net filled with snips of her own hair. She called this a *rat*. After carefully pinning her long hair neatly over the rat and anchoring it with large gray pins you would truly believe she possessed a full head of hair. No one would have guessed her fine hair was thinning with age.

Aunt Elizabeth would plan a trip for us on the trolley to East Liberty. We would visit the zoo in Highland Park then participate in her favorite sport of window-shopping. Elizabeth had great disdain for the automobile. We would cross the busy streets in East Liberty against the traffic lights. She would simply wave her arm at the motorist and shout, "Stay back there." Fortunately, they did!

Neither Elizabeth nor Adelia spent money on ready-made clothing. Adelia had a Singer sewing machine with a push foot pedal. This she rocked back and forth with terrific speed. Every dress was made using the same basic pattern. Variety was achieved by the use of fabric design and treatment around the dress collar. Fabrics for the dresses were carefully selected from Kaufman's department store. One of their permanent residents was a delightful gentleman who was the buyer of fabrics and sewing notions. Mr. Gerald would inform Adelia of bargains in his department. For one camp session Adelia and I took the trolley to downtown Pittsburgh. I had the privilege of meeting Mr. Gerald in his impressive office. That experience may have planted a seed in my subconscious mind since my first career was as a department store buyer for John Wanamaker in Philadelphia. The camp experience produced many delightful memories and much wisdom. These will be addressed in the second installment of this trilogy.

Educating a Country Girl-Part Two

The Lansdale sisters rented rooms to interesting persons. One couple stands out in my memory. It was Mr. Smith, a single man, and his mother, Mrs. Smith, a widow. Mr. Smith was a lawyer with substantial income. He needed a safe and comfortable place for his mother to live her remaining days on earth. She was ninety something. She was very frail and could no longer walk. Mr. Smith hired several nurses to work shifts around the clock. The nurses wore stiff white uniforms with starched caps and significant black bands on the flap. Every need was addressed for Mrs. Smith. The Lansdale sisters provided three meals daily not only for Mrs. Smith but the attending nurses as well. Mrs. Smith could not manage to cut her food so the nurse on duty would pull the food into small bite size pieces. The food was placed in the old lady's mouth. She would roll it around and chew it with the few remaining teeth in her mouth. One bite would take as much as ten minutes to process and swallow. Thus well over an hour would be spent on meal times. Mrs. Smith was always kept immaculate in appearance. Her long thin white hair was carefully combed since her aging head was very tender. Then the nurses would loosely braid her hair and create a diadem like appearance on the top of her head. She was always dressed in white. Mr. Smith had his mother's many dresses sent out to a nearby Chinese laundry for fastidious cleaning and pressing.

The room rented by the Smiths was the largest bedroom in the house and had once been the master bedroom for the family who owned the house. The room spanned the entire front of the house with three large windows. Mrs. Smith relished being wheeled in her chair to one of the windows so she could enjoy watching the street. It was a quiet tree lined street that ran perpendicular on the prestigious Fifth Avenue. From the Lansdale home, one had to walk only two blocks to board a Fifth Avenue Trolley. There were few automobiles using Ivy Street but considerable amount of foot traffic. In late afternoon college students returned to rented rooms in the neighborhood from classes at the

University of Pittsburgh. Midmorning, homemakers would dress smartly and enjoy a shopping trip to downtown Pittsburgh. Others would walk toward the Shady Side market area two blocks the opposite way from Fifth Avenue to replenish their food supplies. The Smith's room had a large fireplace, a cozy asset in the winter giving Mrs. Smith another thing to watch. Mrs. Smith was a well-educated woman whose eyesight was about half the strength of former years. The nurses would sit beside her and read books to her. This was a delight for her. However, her favorite pastime was having a visitor. During my stay Aunt Elizabeth would check with the nurse on duty to determine the appropriate time for my formal visit. When I entered the room Mrs. Smith would greet me with "Hello, Child. Come sit beside me and tell me about your activities." She was interested in every detail. I was very shy and would sit quietly in the chair beside her. She took the initiative in the conversations. She was armed with many questions. Her mind was clear and inquisitive. To a young person, her white dress, braid diadem, veined and wizened hands were a bit scary. She would not allow the nurses to trim her fingernails. They grew long and curved under giving her hands a frightful appearance. I have wondered if perhaps the trimming of the nails were a painful experience for her old joints and bones.

Her son, Mr. Smith, was a dignified man in his seventies. He always wore a black suit with a vest and a somber tie. That was the uniform for a successful lawyer of the day. His shoes were always black, smartly polished and several inches above his ankles, tied with long crisscross shoestrings. His hair was nearly white and well-manicured.

Sometimes he would arrive while I was still visiting Mrs. Smith. He was clearly delighted to see me. He would bow ever so slightly while shaking my hand in greeting. He always told me how very much his mother appreciated my visits.

Mrs. Smith had a double bed with four posters, a white spread and sheets. Beside her bed was her wheelchair. A large night-stand which housed the many utensils needed for her care was on the opposite side of the bed. There were several rockers placed strategically about the room. On the opposite side of the massive room was Mr. Smith's day bed. He also had a desk on which he piled his legal papers. Sitting beside the desk was his fat leather valise. He carried it to and from his law office daily. This was no small feat. I am sure it weighed in excess of twenty pounds. Perhaps that was part of the reason he appeared to be physically fit. His posture was tall and straight. He walked with a firm stride. His chin was held straight. To a young person he was a bit intimidating. However, the kindness in his eyes soon made you comfortable in his presence.

In the center of the room was a round table with a vase of fresh flowers. Mr. Smith had them replenished on a regular basis. Near Mrs. Smith's bed was a medium sized table with wheels. This is where the Lansdale sisters would place the trays of food that were delivered daily. When Mrs. Smith was finished eating, the nurse on duty would wheel the table to the hallway immediately outside the door.

As I grew closer to college age, Mrs. Smith moved closer to her exit from earth. One night she simply never awoke from her sleep. Upon her demise,

Mr. Smith no longer rented the room. I have often wondered where he decided to live. It was not evident that he had any siblings, spouse, or children. Perhaps he soon followed his mother in crossing the river. That could very well have been the case since he was in his seventies. Not all persons inherit the long life of a parent. How very blessed Mrs. Smith was to have had a son that was able to provide such great care and remained by her side to supervise the entire process. Not many persons of that day could afford nurses round the clock, home cooked food delivered thrice daily, fresh flowers, ample supplies of white dresses laundered in Chinese laundries. Perhaps the greatest blessing of all in the Smiths' lives was the fact that two industrious and caring spinsters owned a lovely home and a room with a view.

Educating a Country Girl-Part Three

Occasionally, as in any business, the Lansdale sisters were faced with an unusual challenge. A young professional woman visited them looking for a room. Most of their renters were long term and vacancies were rare. At this particular time, however, they had a person vacating the front room on the third floor. The young woman, Miss Jones, had learned about this through a friend. Ordinarily, the Lansdale sisters would check references and finding no problem would take Miss Jones as the new third floor resident. This time, although the references were satisfactory, there was a new angle to consider. Miss Jones had a precocious five-year-old daughter. Jane had the combined energy of three five-year-olds. Miss Jones, her mother, had an avant-garde approach to single motherhood. She wanted Jane to be a free spirit. Jane needed little encouragement in this area of her personality. I have often wondered what spark ignited the decision to accept this duo.

After moving into the third floor room, Miss Jones promptly resumed her professional career leaving Jane alone all day with the two spinsters. There were no "day care" centers at this time in this section of Pittsburgh. When Jane and her mother arrived, Aunt Adelia was about 53-years-old. Aunt Elizabeth was seven years older than Adelia and blessed with a crown of glory. Her hair was white and thick with no strands of color. Neither of the women had good qualifications for the proper dealing with a child. When Aunt Adelia, worked in Uniontown for the Rosenbaum family, as a servant, there were no children in this household according to the census. The Rosenbaum family consisted of Mr. and Mrs. Rosenbaum and one of their elderly parents who had emigrated from Germany.

Jane promptly established herself in the total house. She had a loud deep voice, almost masculine in pitch. She would run up and down the two flights of stairs making firm stomps as she landed on each tread. She quickly began calling the sisters "Adelia and Elizabeth." Both of the Lansdale women stood their ground insisting Jane address them as Miss Adelia and Miss Elizabeth. Perhaps it was the unity between them that caused Jane to change her salutations.

Of course, Jane followed them all about the house as they performed their tasks. Aunt Adelia insisted Jane sit on a chair in the kitchen while food was being prepared. This was no small feat for Jane to obey. She wanted to explore the kitchen gadgets, pots, pans....yes even the coal bucket used to keep the mammoth black stove hot for cooking the many pies, cakes, cookies, and meat roasts that were needed on a daily basis to supply the meals for their paying guests. I can only guess that Aunt Adelia bribed her with the promise of one of her fabulous donuts or cookies.

I visited the Lansdale sisters one summer when Jane was living in their home. The girls thought I would be a good foil to the rambunctious Jane. Although I was about 14-years-old at that time, Jane wore me out completely. She would grab my hand and pull me to a new mysterious nook in the house that she had discovered. "I don't think we should be roaming all over the house," I would tell Jane. She would respond firmly, "Miss Elizabeth won't mind." Need I tell you that my training at home was *"keep quiet, stay where you are told, and play only with those things that were approved."* For Jane, those rules were like being in a foreign culture. Each day during that week's visit I would check the large Grandfather clock in the hall to see how many hours were left before Jane's mother, Miss Jones, would return. She always spent time with Jane but it was in the third floor room. Serenity would return to the large home on Ivy Street when Jane followed her mother to their rented room on the third floor.

The Lansdale sisters managed to survive for one year with daily "Now, Jane...no, Jane." Then Miss Jones enrolled Jane in school at the age of six. Miss Jones and Jane lived at Ivy Street for several years. During that time the two Lansdale women were strong influences in Jane's formation. She was taught social graces and respect for authority. These lessons were laced with love and care. This was not lost on

Jane. She grew to love the elderly ladies as though they were her Grandmothers. In some respects they were. Jane kept in contact with them for many years. Aunt Elizabeth died in Pittsburgh. Aunt Adelia sold the lovely house and moved to an apartment in Brownsville, Pennsylvania to be near her only living sibling, William Preston Lansdale. Adelia continued to receive letters and pictures from Jane. She also had one or two personal visits. By that time, Jane was married and had her own family. Although it was never verbalized to me, I believe Jane became the grandchild the Lansdale sisters were not able to have. We could call the turn of events a "Win, Win Situation."

* * * *

The encounters at the "summer camp" gave me insights more precious than simple refinements of society. They were windows into the lives of real people and their personal attempts to meet challenges common to being human. I received inspiration from each person.

God's Creatures
"relationships with nature and humans"

Sleep comes often now. While sitting in a chair, the sensation of imminent loss of consciousness forces me to seek a supported position for my head. But this state of affairs was not in existence 86 years ago. At that time my body was full of bountiful energy. There was so much to see, to explore, to hear, and to learn. Why would anyone want to waste time taking an afternoon nap? But conventional wisdom of the day was that growing little girls, age three, needed a rest every afternoon. There are no memories of fussing with Mom about taking a nap. Perhaps I knew even then that a child never said NO to a parent.

Grandma Lansdale was at our house spending the afternoon with me. Mom and Dad were away. That was a rare occasion. My parents did not use "babysitters". Never did learn why they were away that day but it must have been important. Grandma Florence Lansdale was a wonderful lady. She made the best ginger cookies to ever touch a child's lips. She was the one who made a little bucket for me out of a tin can laced with bailing twin for handles. She with her large gallon bucket and I with my tin can would wonder out to the woods on Grandfather's farm. She knew where the best black berries could be found. It was in the deep shade far into the thickest part of the briar patch. There if you stooped low and looked up you would see clusters of blackberries the size of Grandma's thumb. If you popped one into your mouth the berry would release its succulent juices giving out the most glorious flavor a three-year-old mind could fathom. Grandma would pop one in her mouth, savor the pleasure, then look at me with eyes full of mischief and say "we just canned those two berries on the spot." This would be followed by a laugh that came from somewhere deep inside her body.

Florence was the Grandma that I enjoyed. My other Grandma, Agnes Winslow was nice but she could not hear a sound. She would lean down and look into your face to read your lips. Sometimes she spoke in a whisper, and sometimes with a strange loud sound. Typhoid fever had left Grandma Winslow deaf, so she could not moderate her voice with the ear as normal persons. As a three-year-old child, this made me feel uncomfortable. So it was time with Grandma Lansdale that I looked forward to with great expectation.

As most children will tell you, Grandmas' are truly special. Florence Lansdale was no exception. In the afternoon after a hard morning's work in the garden, or after several hours in the hot kitchen baking bread, she would take a few minutes to sit with me on the porch swing. We would both delight in the cooling breeze generated by the swings motion.

Sometimes we would sing together. Other times when Grandma Lansdale was busy with farm chores I would wonder along the line of green gage plum trees, looking for a ripe plum that had fallen to the ground. The game was to find one that recently fallen before the ants smelled the sweet nectar and claimed it. I knew the green gage plums were something to cherish because of Florence's green gage plum pies. In all my 86 years I have never tasted any pie that would compare with those plum pies.

When appropriate, Florence would take me along when she gathered the eggs. This was fun to one who loved discovery. The chickens on the Grandpa's farm were given free range. In order to enjoy eggs for dinner, we had to search for their nests. The chickens were creative creatures. God gave them uncanny insight for placing their nests in the most unlikely spots. What a delight for me when I found one that Grandma had not seen.

With all these wonderful memories of Grandma, it was a surprise when she told me it was time to take a nap that afternoon as she filled in for Mom and Dad. "I don't want to take a nap, Grandma." I announced. "Come, child, take off your dress so you don't get it all wrinkled as you sleep," she said taking my little hand firmly. I went along with her but my lower lip protruded a bit. She draped my little red print dress neatly over a chair back, adjusted the blanket over me, walked softly to the door, and pulled it closed behind her.

I lay in the bed awake. I knew I must stay there. Mom had taught me that little girls did what they were told. So I spent time looking about at the wall paper, the pictures on the wall, the furniture, the quilt on my bed. When that activity became boring, I started using my imagination. I thought of walks along the stream in the woods near our little rented house, of the wild sweet Williams growing in the neighbor's meadow, of the dogwood trees with their fragrant petals, of the birds singing lustily to each other. While in my delightful reverie the door opened slightly; Florence whispered loud enough for me to hear, "Get to sleep."

"I can't sleep, Grandma. I am wide awake."
Silence followed. The door closed and I continued my
day dreams. Sometime later the door opened again.
When Florence saw that I was still lying there with my
eyes open she approached the bed. She had something
in her hand. As she got closer to me I could hear a low
pitch buzzing. Grandma was holding between her
thumb and forefinger a live wasp. "You see this?" she
asked with a forceful voice, one not at all familiar. "If
you are not asleep within the next five minutes, I will
let it crawl over your face."

I muffled a wild scream and pulled the cover
over my face. I could feel my heart thudding rapidly
in my chest. The tears streamed down my face but I
held back the sobs. They were silent tears. Mom did
not permit me to cry. Grandma would not be pleased
with tears either. I used the sheet to absorb the salty
liquid on my face. It became very warm under the
covers since my breathing that matched the pace of
my heart had created a small furnace. But that proved
to be a blessing. The warmth and the darkness under
the covers provided a sleep-inducing potion. The next
thing I remember was Mom telling me it was time for
supper. You can be sure nothing was said to either
Mom or Dad about the wasp. As an only child, I had
early learned that the less said to adults, the better the
situation.

I often wonder how Grandma Florence found
the wasp. How did she catch it without being stung? I
suspect this was one of the many practical things her
mother, Rozilla, had passed along to her children.
Florence's mother was Native American. I am also
thankful that Grandma Lansdale did not allow the
wasp to get too close to my face.

Four years later, at the age of seven, I was playing barefoot in the grass. My foot stepped on a wasp crawling beneath the blades. The sting was ferocious. Not only did it hurt so much that I could not hold the tears and sobs within me, but my foot and leg swelled to five times the normal size. My foot was green and blue. I could not walk on the leg. Dad had to carry me to school for the next week. Mom did not chide me for the tears and sobs this time.

For the ensuing years of my life, I have been wary of the wasp. It has been etched in my mind that it is one of God's mighty, tiny creatures. I have not walked barefoot in the grass since that innocent day. The habit serves me well now. In Northwest Florida where there are many of The Creator's mighty tiny animals, such as black widow spiders, and fire ants who make their home in the grass just outside our new home. Sometimes I ponder this question that cannot be answered. Did the *severe effect* of the animal's sting on my foot have something to do with the sight of the wiggling little beast in Grandmother Florence's hand?

A Small Bundle
"in my arms"

Mama ran our retail dairy. We lived on a farm in Western Pennsylvania. We had fifty cows that needed to be milked and fed night and morning before and after school. There was also the bottling of the milk, loading the truck with crates to be delivered daily, house to house, in towns along the Monongahela River. This required long and hard work each day. Mother wanted me to learn that habit. I did. Mama also wanted me to learn other valuable lessons for life.

One Saturday, she and I were riding along in the large white dairy truck embellished with green lettering "Hall's Guernsey Dairy." The dairy logo was a orange cow's face in an oval frame [Guernsey cows are orange and white in color.] Hall's Dairy served customers in seven river towns. We had finished delivery to California and Coal Centre. Our next stop was Elco. This day Mom made a new turn and drove up a winding narrow road along a creek with rapidly flowing crystal clear water.

"You must have picked up a new customer, Mom." I said. I admired her. She was not only a well-informed dairy farmer, but a good business manager and super sales person.

"I want to show you something", she replied.

Soon she stopped the truck. We were in Elco Hollow. That is what the local folk called this area of nearly vertical hills on either side. The narrow valley had almost no flat land. A one lane dirt road had been created in the center and ran parallel to the creek. Dotted here and there along the hollow were small shanty houses. Mom told me to stay in the truck. She picked up a half gallon bottle of milk and got out of the truck. She carefully stepped along a wooden plank that spanned the creek. The ten inch wide board had been laid down without any attachment. Each end rested on the stone studded banks of the creek. The plank swayed with each step Mom took as she carefully walked. She went inside the small black gray clapboard shanty. Straggly weeds filled the front yard. The window blinds were pulled down revealing several tears and rips. They were yellowed with age and flecked here and there with brown water stains.

In about ten minutes Mom came out the door of the house carrying a small bundle. She was followed by a frail, thin woman who walked gingerly in her bare feet to the wooden plank. She leaned on a sagging post while watching Mother carry the bundle across the creek to our truck.

Mom opened the truck door and placed the bundle on my lap. I nearly choked from the putrid odor. I had never smelled anything like this before. Inside the bundle was a tiny baby wrapped in a woman's slip. He made faces but no sound. His little body moved only slightly.

"This little baby is starving," Mom said. "His mommy is so undernourished and weak she cannot nurse him. She, too, is starving. The baby is too weak to cry. It is so weak it can hardly move. This is our new customer. We are going to provide milk without charge for this infant and his mommy every day. I want you to remember this baby. I want you to always try to do what you can to help those who need you." I have often wondered how Mom found the little child and its mother. How did she know about the situation in this remote area of town? Many times I would discover that my mother was quietly helping a family. She did not talk about these activities. So, in addition to learning a work ethic, I learned to do for the "least." Mom taught me to see God in many places. Her actions are seared into my being.

* * * * *

God was in Mary's baby for whom we celebrate Christmas. He was also in the poor starving mother's baby. A major teaching given to those who followed the Jewish Rabbi called Jesus was direct. The instruction did not require extended collegiate study. The guideline is ever fresh and relative. "What you do to the least, you do to Me." I left the farm that fall to attend Penn State University. The memory of that tiny child in my arms will never be forgotten. One person offering milk for free enabled another person to live.

Christmas, Flossie, Pneumonia
"child's viewpoint"

Mom and Dad had moved my black iron bed into the living room because the bedroom did not have any source of heat. The living room had a stove that burned coal. Coal was a free source of heat. My parents picked the left over pieces from the local slagheap. This was permitted, sort of like the Biblical gleaning principle where poor folk were permitted to gather what was left from the harvest. The coal bits were left over from the machinery that separated the coal and rock after it was mined from the ground.

It was warm near the stove but cold in the corners of the room. Mother placed two thick quilts hand made from free men's suit samples on my twin size bed. Snow was over the knee deep all over the rolling hills and wooded country in Western Pennsylvania. Overnight temps hovered at about 10 degrees above zero. Warmth was a concern because I had pneumonia. Mom regularly placed fresh poultices on my chest to ease the breathing difficulty. I was four-years-old.

A fresh fir tree had been placed in the corner across from my bed so I could lie there and look at it. I loved the lights. I still enjoy Christmas lights at 86 years old. My Father had carefully placed long silver foil ice cycles on the tree. They were lovely at night when they reflected the tree lights. During the day I preferred the ice cycles hanging from the roof outside the three room rented house. Several icicles were visible to me as I lay in bed looking out the window. Each day they grew longer and larger as the sun melted a bit of the two feet of snow on the roof. As the winds blew and early darkness arrived the water would freeze to add wonderful layers. You could see the layers. Each reflected the light in its own unique way.

Christmas Eve was tough to get through for the little family of three in the rented house in rural Long Branch. I coughed a lot and worked hard to force the air in and out of my lung chambers. Mom and Dad were not only concerned about my health but how to allow the miracle of Santa Claus to happen in the same room. Finally in the wee hours, I stopped coughing long enough to sleep. Quickly my parents slipped wrapped packages under the tree.

When the light appeared I was awake and called out, "Mommy, did Santa come?"

I was too weak to get out of bed. I could only see the top part of the tree. None of the presents were visible.

"Oh, my yes," Mom assured me. Turning to my father she said," Daddy show Oceola what Santa brought." Dad quickly walked to the tree and kneeling down held up a box wrapped in red print paper. There was no bow since money was too tight for frivolity. He placed it on my bed. "Daddy, will you open it for me?" I asked. I was too tired and weak to hold the box. Dad tore open the paper and opened the box. It had in it a little plate, cup, and saucer. When I saw it I began to cry and with the congestion in my lungs started to choke. Mom jumped up from her chair. "What's the matter? Why are you crying? Don't you like the dishes?"

Between the coughs I managed to get out these words. "Santa did not bring me a baby doll." My mother quickly replied. "Daddy, see what else is under the tree." This time Daddy walked over to my bed with a beautiful baby doll dressed in a long white christening gown. I pulled the doll close to me. "I shall name her Flossie." I sighed with joy and closed my eyes promptly drifting into a deep sleep.

As an old woman I think of "Flossie" and would actually like to hold the doll once again. As a young married woman I gave the doll to another little girl, Bonita, who is my double cousin's child. Bonita was the only little girl in our family at the time. If the moment of gifting could take place again I would have sought out a little girl in a hospital ward at Christmas time whose parents could afford very little, like my own parents. "Flossie" was tossed away by Bonita whose parents gave her many gifts. Hand-me-downs were not favorite toys.

But I do hold the doll in my heart as though it were yesterday. It does not matter that "Flossie" was tossed. She fulfilled her purpose by making a very sick child feel happy and contented one Christmas long ago.

* * * * *

At the time that I gave my precious Flossie to my second cousin I thought I was doing the right thing. Bonita was a relative. Over the years I may now have a glimpse of what Jesus meant when He asked this question. "Who is my family?" You might want to read in your Bible once again the statements recorded in Matthew 12:48-50. Many thoughts come to my mind. I ask myself what this question means to me. There are few relatives remaining in my family. And yet my family is prolific in my memory, my present experiences, and will be in the future hours and moments to come.

Newell's Mystique
"years ago"

As Mom eased our Model T Ford down the slope to board the river ferry, Gabby emerged from the weather grayed wooden shack. He waddled toward our car on his severely bowed legs. His mouth, as usual, was spread apart in a smile revealing several missing teeth. Now and then he paused, turned his head slightly and issued a huge spray of dark tobacco juice from his lips. When he reached the front window on the driver's side, Mom cranked down the car window half way and handed him a quarter. Gabby tipped his black Captain's hat and bowed slightly. As the old man slowly made his way back to the shack, Mom eased the Model T to the point where the ferryboat's slanted planks touched the riverbank. She waited while Gabby started the huge engine that ran the ferryboat's pulley. The sound reminded me of a thrashing machine engine on Grandfather's farm at harvest time. It was difficult to have any conversation with the motor running.

At the appropriate time Gabby slowly proceeded to the ferryboat, then, motioned for Mom to drive upon the deck. I was always fearful she would push the gas pedal too forcefully and drive right over the opposite end of the ferry and into the river. The only thing preventing this fearful scenario was a thin chain strung across the landing planks at the opposite end of the rickety boat plus my mother's driving skill. Mind you, I did not perceive Elizabeth Lansdale as a poor motorist. But I had heard stories of other motorists who had managed to plunge right into the river. If they could make a mistake, could Mom do the same thing?

Once our car was parked in the middle of the boat, Mom turned off the engine and pulled on the brake. Gabby now attached another chain to the back of the ferryboat. He pulled down a long lever about as tall as he was. The ropes that held the pulley tightened and gradually we began to move across the river. If a river steamer had recently gone up or down the river, the resulting waves would rock the ferryboat pulling it off course and away from the target landing on the opposite side of the river. I heard the groans and squeaks of the ropes and pulley. What if the ropes snapped? The ferryboat would then drift down stream. I knew that lock number four was just around the river bend. What would keep the boat from cascading over the concrete walls of the dam? Once time in the past I had voiced my fears to Mother. She quickly instructed me to avoid letting my imagination get the best of me. After that I simply kept my "what if" thoughts to myself.

After about fifteen minutes the ferry bumped into the steep road on the opposite side of the river. Gabby had a helper who remained on the Newell side. If the ferry missed its mark on the road, the strong young lad would throw a rope with a hook onto the railing and lean against it to align the landing plank with the road. Today was a perfect landing. The helper unfastened the chain in front of our car so that we could drive up the steep hill into Newell. I was always fascinated by the helper's shelter. It resembled an outhouse. Sometimes the door was open. I could see an old broken stuffed armchair minus its legs. A dirty tattered quilt lay across it. On winter days the helper wrapped the quilt around him to keep warm. There was no other provision for heat in the tiny building. On summer days you could get a good dose of pungent odor emanating from the other side of the flimsy shack. It had a door that opened into the bladder release compartment. The compartment leaned against the front of the building.

I always relaxed when the Model T managed to ascend the steep road from the Monongahela River to the plateau of the town of Newell. Now the fun part of the Newell visit began. We stopped at a white clapboard house in the shape of an oblong. It was the residence of the Gibson Family. Mr. and Mrs. Kenneth Gibson were friends of my parents. They often visited us on the farm and enjoyed a long dinner with much laughter. The Gibson's had an only child. Kenny Gibson Junior was about four years older than I. He later left Newell and enrolled in the Pittsburgh Mortuary Science School to become an undertaker. I could never understand why any boy would select this particular profession. However, I am sure his family never lacked for funds even in bad economic times.

Dad and Kenneth Gibson Senior worked on the Pennsylvania and Lake Erie Railroad. Kenneth Senior was a conductor. He made regular trips to Pittsburgh with the steam engine pulling several miles of railcars filled with coal from mine trestles along the river. Travel time was long since the railroad tracks passed through the center of river towns. Long trains could not stop quickly due to the heavy weight. Sometimes the company attached a second steam engine to the rear of the train to assist with the braking process.

My father was a coal hoist operator at the company's roundhouse. It was always a treat to visit the round house. Mom and I watched as two railroad workers unlatched huge iron and wood doors, pulled them open to allow a steam engine to enter the round building. The engine remained on railroad tracks that were built right into the building. In the center of the round house was a wooden circle with the circumference about four feet longer than the steam engine. A motor operator moved the circle slowly until the tracks on the circle lined up exactly with the tracks on which the train engine had entered the building. Then the engineer would lean out of the window with one hand on the ledge, the other holding the lever that governed the forward movement of the steam belching behemoth. Ever so slowly the long arm of the engine glided forward and back moving the wheels. Once the steam engine was positioned properly, all systems were shut down.

A team of specialized mechanics entered the round house. Some climbed up to the conductor's box. Others inspected the wheels and levers. Still others descended some stairs to long tunnels beneath the engine. From this vantage point they inspected many moving parts. Using tin pails with very long handles they poured oil the joints. I loved every minute of the spectacle. After several hours the engine inspection and servicing were completed. Once again huge doors, this time on the opposite side of the round house were opened to allow the aligning of the tracks. Whistles blew with various pitches. Coals smoldering in the firebox were fanned to life by giant bellows. The fireman shoveled tiny nuggets of coal, known as slack, on top of the red coals. Steam begin to build up in the chambers filled with water and hiss fiercely. When the correct pressure was reached, the conductor once again leaned out the window in the same position, watching the dispatch man as he waved his lantern signaling a "go."

Dad seemed to enjoy showing Mother and I the activity in the round house. His fellow workers always make a fuss over Clifford's little girl. I suspect that if Dad dared to be forthright with the men he would have confessed that he was proud that his daughter was so interested in men's toys.

Sometimes after work Dad would take Mom and I into the large brick two story building in Newell that resembled a hotel. In fact it was a hotel of sorts. The conductors and their crew would sleep overnight there until the steam engines were serviced and were ready for the next run between the Allegheny Mountains and Pittsburgh. Women in white uniforms worked in the main floor kitchen to provide warm hearty breakfast for the railroad personnel.

The Pittsburgh and Lake Erie Railroad and the Chemical Plant were the reasons Newell existed. Houses were homes for the many workers. There was a Catholic church built in the little river town. It still stands today although few of Newell's twenty first century residents adhere to that faith. Mass is still proclaimed and the clanging bells in the tower reverberate from the hills surrounding the Newell plateau.

Last summer as I stood at River Heights Tavern and photographed the serene beauty of the river town of Newell I remembered Dad and Mom. Dad crossed the Monongahela River twice each day for forty-eight years as an employee of the railroad. How did he manage to endure the tedium, the bitter cold winters, the prison-like existence of work eat, sleep, with no vacation?

How did my parents keep on keeping on?

Perspective on Brownsville
"only true value lasts"

Mom and I had a ritual. Twice monthly the
workers living in the towns along the Monongahela
River were given an envelope with cash. Most of our
customers would then leave a note in the empty milk
bottles sitting at their front doors with this message.
"I want to pay my bill." Mother would tally the
amount due for each individual customer on a small
form then hand it to me. It was my duty to knock on
the door and collect the money. This was fine with me.
Occasionally several of our customers would neglect
to offer to pay their bills. I was then instructed to
knock on the door and ask, "Do you want to pay
today?" Being shy and passive, this was an
uncomfortable chore. Mom, being a parent who
maintained discipline, did not give me the option of
saying, "I don't want to do this. It embarrasses me."
An obedient child, even if an only child, always did
what they were told. So I doggedly walked up to the
door and asked "Do you want to pay today?"
Sometimes the lady of the house would respond, "Not
today." Others would say, "Stop by next payday." A
few homemakers would pull back their curtains at the
window, see me standing there and never answer the
door. I wonder if they knew I could see what was
happening? In those days adults sometimes thought
children missed things. It makes me chuckle to recall
how very much I observed and knew about many
situations. At the time, however, it made me feel small
and very insignificant.

Finally the collection part of the ritual would
be completed. For the final stage, Mom would drive to
Brownsville. She had a bank account at the First

National Bank of Brownsville. This was the place she deposited all receipts from our retail milk route. Sometimes we would visit the brand new, large to a child's eyes, super market. Mom would carefully select items to supplement our garden produce and store of jars of home canned food.

On other visits we would stop in the Five and Ten Cent Store. It was a delight to roam the aisles looking at all the goodies. A special attraction for me was the collection of cut out books. They cost about 5 pennies and gave me hours of pleasure as I carefully moved my bunny scissors (instruments with rounded edges) along the lines printed at the edge of the dolls and their assortments of clothing. As I moved along in school the interest in cut out books was replaced by interest in extra clothes for my dolls. Mom was more stringent with her "okay to buy" since doll clothes cost considerably more than cut out books.

Now and then Mom would take me into the upper class stores in Brownsville. The two that remain vividly in my memory was Kart's and Goldstein's. These stores carried clothing for women, teens and preteens. My girlfriends from Centerville often shopped with their mothers in these stores. They would casually comment, "This outfit comes from Karts." I knew this was a form of bragging. Of course it exists today with designer labels. It is insidious. Those who have not, feel less valuable than those who have. I knew we could not afford the lovely things shown in the windows and did not feel resentment toward my Mother. I was aware that Mom did the best she could, worked very hard, and was frugal. Somehow I considered this a virtue and maintain this attitude to this moment.

The most painful recollection I have of our forays into Karts and Goldstein's is the treatment we received. Remember that the last half of our ritual took place as we were going home from making milk deliveries. Each of us wore jeans. Today women of high social statue would not look askew at this attire. However, in the thirties and forties, women of means never wore jeans. Mom would purchase men's jeans sizes too large for each of us. She would then remove the fly front replacing it with a single side-zipper seam. These altered garments combined with a tailored blouse became our uniforms. When we entered the prestigious establishments of Karts and Goldstein's both store personnel and customers would treat us as though we were invisible. Mother would be forced to persist in her request for assistance. There was very little self-service for shoppers at that time. Most of the goods for sale were folded in drawers with glass fronts or hung inside cabinets with glass doors. Only a clerk could access them.

I knew the reason for the snubs. Mother did, too. It was primarily due to the fact we were wearing jeans. It was also due to the fact that we were not part of society's elite. We never talked about this. We simply finished our ritual and went home.

As the years passed my parent's dairy became very successful financially. Mom could walk into any store and purchase any thing she wanted. In my Senior High School Yearbook I was voted the best dressed in my class. That was nice since I always was interested in clothes beginning with those cut out books.

After graduation from Centerville High School I matriculated to one of the prestigious "big ten universities." Just before graduation from Centerville, a wise teacher call me to her office and admonished me to pursue extra-curricular activities and have fun in the college experience with less emphasis on serious study. Did I follow her excellent advice? Yes, Yes. And Yes!

The result was that I won recognition awards and articles were written about the local girl from Centerville in the Brownsville Telegraph. Mom reported to me in her letters that Mrs. Goldstein, herself now insisted on helping her shop. She went on and on about my achievements. At that time in my life's journey I was furious. "Mom! Why do you even shop in those stores?" "You must not hold a grudge, Oceola," she would say. She was right of course. It was difficult for me to maintain a forgiving attitude. I hated the hypocrisy and the snobbery.

* * * * *

But now with the passage of time I have a new and hopefully clearer vision of the nitty gritty of this story. The shopping streets of Brownsville have literally no buildings that are open for business. Every shop has its windows boarded up. The shop owners are no longer alive. Yes hypocrisy and snobbery still exists in society. However, I can see the big picture now. I have learned the truth of storing treasure that lasts. I have learned that you can enjoy deep happiness with very little material things. I have learned that true friends are those with whom you share precious memories of living through both the good and the bad times. I have learned that valuable friends are those people who take the time to get to know the person wearing the clothes whether the outfit is the latest trend or a careful purchase from a local thrift store. I am thankful for these memories. They are a mixture of pain and satisfaction. They make life colorful and worthwhile.

Who did it?
"the unexplained"

Most people today believe that angels are people who do nice things for others. People who come along at the appropriate time to help a person who is in great need emotionally, mentally, physically, or even spiritually. I do believe people are used by God to help others. I believe in synchronicity...a word coined by the famous Swiss psychologist, Carl Jung. He wrote extensively about events and people coming together at the most appropriate moment. He discovered that pattern many times in his work with clients.

When we look at scripture we get a different point of view regarding angels. All three major religious faiths, Judaism, Christianity, and Islam have holy writings that tell of angelic beings visiting the earth.

Jesus implied that each person has an angel assigned to him or her. You might want to read Matthew 18:10 in your own Bible. I have never seen an angel, nor have I ever had a dramatic encounter in which another human being could be classified as an *angel*. I HAVE met and seen many wonderful people who do outstanding things for others. Many people have done nice things to me and for me and I thank God for them.

My most memorable experiences are of a mysterious nature. They are happenings that cannot be explained in logical terms. The first that comes to my mind occurred when I was about 11-years-old. At that time I was living on a farm in the hills of Western

Pennsylvania. Being an only child all my extra time was needed to assist with farm chores. I wanted some money of my own to buy gifts. My mother did not approve of giving children allowances. When I mentioned that all my friends at school received allowances, my mother said "a child should not be paid for doing chores. That is part of their duty." Her tone of voice indicated that the matter was closed for further discussion. Inside I felt sad, for I truly wanted to present gifts to my Mom. Often I would go shopping with my best friend, Anita Rollins. She had a weekly allowance. She carefully stashed it away in a drawer in her room to purchase nice things for her parents. It is interesting that I do not recall her ever buying something for herself.

As an aside, Anita is still a dear friend today, spanning over sixty years of friendship. In addition to her unselfish personality Anita has many other wonderful attributes that make her a cherished friend.

What does a young girl do when she cannot get a job, is too young and too busy working for her family? I resorted to the only thing I could think of…deep agonizing petition to God. "Please help me God. You know my heart. You know how I ache inside to be able to give Mom a present for Mother's day."

Early Friday morning after farm chores were finished I quickly dressed, scooped up my lunch, school books and scurried out the door. I had to walk about a half mile along a county road to a school bus stop. About half way to the destination I looked down and saw a pair of ladies gloves. I stooped to pick them up wondering who dropped them. Holding them in my hands I realized they were brand new. They had been lying on the edge of the road. There was not even a tiny speck of dirt on them. They were made of luxuriously soft tan leather. They would be a perfect gift for my Mother. I was not sure that they would fit but the size looked promising. I carefully tucked them in my geography book. It was large enough to completely cover them.

I was so excited it was an effort to keep my mind on classroom activities that day. I knew Mom had no pretty gloves to wear. These would go with all her special outfits. Women wore gloves in those days. It was considered a necessary part of a well-dressed lady's ensemble.

The next day, Saturday, I rummaged in our farmhouse attic. Mom was very frugal and kept an assortment of boxes and used ribbons along with old clothing to be cut up for quilts, cleaning cloths, aprons, and other various uses. I found a suitable box and some red ribbon to tie around the box. Then I hid the gift under my bed. After breakfast and the morning dairy duties were completed I proudly presented the gift to my Mother. This is your "Mother's Day Gift". She was so shocked she said nothing for a moment or two. Then she asked how I got the gloves. I told her about finding them on my way to school. Since I had never dared lie to her she did not accuse me of stealing nor did she question my explanation.

"Do they fit?" I asked all the while praying hard that they would. She carefully picked them up and slid one on her tiny hand. It fit like a custom design.

"These are a wonderful gift, Oceola," Mom said. "They will hide my calloused ugly hands when we go out to special places."

* * * * *

No one had heard my prayer except God for it was not spoken aloud. The lovely gloves were simply there at the right place and at the perfect time. Was this an accident that Dr. Jung would call synchronicity? Did a _passerby_ accidentally drop them? People did not usually walk along county roads since the distance to towns did not lend itself to walking. There were no other houses close to our farm house. Were the gloves placed along my path to the bus stop by an invisible angel in answer to a child's urgent prayer? The answer will always be one of the mysteries of my life. Perhaps I will know the truth when I enter the Great Unknown with its angelic hosts. Meanwhile I am content to know that God hears my prayers even though He often answers with silence, but many times with complete surprises.

The Art of Milking a Cow
"advice for city slickers"

Anytime you begin a major activity you must prepare. Preparation for City Slickers is of major importance. You would never approach a cow wearing sandals. The animal usually weighs between 700 to 800 pounds. She will often step about moving her body from side to side. I recommend protective footwear, preferably the steel toe variety.

While you are milking, your head will be very close to the cow. Her body odor will quickly be absorbed into your own hair. Therefore, you should tie a scarf securely around your hair making sure it is entirely covered. The only exception to this suggestion would be for totally bald men. Now top the scarf with a baseball cap turned backward. You must keep the front of your face free to see clearly so you can meet any challenge from the cow quickly.

Now slather your face with heavy cold cream that rests on the surface of the skin and can be easily wiped off. Safety goggles should be slipped on next. There is an important reason for this procedure. During the night as the cow is sleeping her tail rests on the ground. The tail is made up of a flexible cartilage and long hair. The hair collects the products of the cow's bathroom activities. When you get near her she will assuredly begin switching her tail. When it hits you it will feel like a leather whip. The products it has collected will be spread mercilessly over your face.

When you are properly dressed for the art of milking you should select a bucket to collect the milk.

It should have a low center of gravity, and be impervious to heavy blows. It should be light in weight so that you can deftly and swiftly pull it away from lightning quick kicks by the cow's foot.

For your first attempt at the art of milking, I would suggest that you distract the animal by presenting her a generous portion of ground corn, wheat, oats, and sorghum. She will be especially attracted to your offering if you include malt, a by-product of whiskey. Be careful. Do not add too much malt. It could make her inebriated.

While she is busy enjoying the delicious snack, quietly and slowly step up to her, speaking her name softly. Be sure to pat her hip gently. Now sit down on your stool. Take a cloth dipped in warm water laced with antiseptic and slowly clean the entire udder. Make sure that that no loose flakes of dirt remain. The cleaning serves two purposes. It enables you to have a clean bucket of milk. Just as important it causes the cow to "let down the milk". Unless the cow relaxes the milk glands you will get only a cupful of milk. At this point place the sturdy bucket directly under the cow's udder.

Now is the time for skillful technique. If you simply squeeze you may get a drop or two. If you squeeze harder you may get some more drops. If you squeeze with all your might you may find yourself lying on your back from a swift kick from the cow's back leg. She knows when you are bumbling around. The proper way is to place your thumb and pointing finger slightly above the teat. Firmly pull the milk down to the edge of the teat then wrap your remaining fingers around it and squeeze. Never do this if you have long fingernails. They will pinch the cow and she will reward you properly but not in a manner that is pleasant. If you want to fill your bucket and not waste the precious milk you must carefully aim the opening of the teat.

Remember to be kind to the farm felines. They work hard to keep the rat and mice population under control and deserve special treats. When they gather around you and sit waiting patiently, direct a flow of milk to their faces. They love this and will spend joyous moments cleaning their faces to get all the drops of milk.

When you have taken all the available milk give yourself a reward. Simply pour the warm milk through a clean white muslin cloth into your cup. You will be surprised to discover that raw fresh milk tastes entirely different from the milk in your supermarket. It is sweet and slightly thick.

You have heard it said "oh, Go milk a duck!" I say to you, if you want to show your courage go milk a cow!

* * * * *

It is a natural thing for most of us to simply take advantage of the myriads of things available to us in this twenty first century. Pause for a minute or two and wonder about all the preparation that is necessary for us to enjoy something as simple as a glass of cold chocolate milk. My husband David was a city slicker when we married. He had the benefits of living in a large metropolitan area. One of his favorite beverages was a glass of cold milk. Can you imagine the culture shock when he was introduced to the process of actually getting milk from its source? When he witnessed the herd of fifty cows entering the barn and walking to their own stalls he hurried to the exit door. As I recall my many episodes of cow milking, even with the assistance of mechanical milking machines, I find my entire self being humbled. I realize things that deserve my gratitude are simply too numerous to count. The science of medicine recognizes that our mental attitudes are a vital factor to our well-being. What is fascinating to me is that the Bible, from cover to cover, teaches us to be humble and thankful. Take another look at First Thessalonians 5:18.

The River
"Thrills and Encounters"

My bare feet were firmly positioned on the square wooden board that was found in a wood scrap pile. The board had been sanded to minimize the danger of splinters. Two large holes were drilled on one side. A long rope was looped through the two holes and attached to the motorboat. I held a sturdy stick in my two hands. The stick was attached to another thinner rope also attached to the motorboat. My knees were bent and my upper torso was leaning forward as my cousin, Dan Lansdale revved the engine. Dan steered the boat toward the middle of the Monongahela River. When the rope was taught between the square board and the boat I experienced liftoff. Miraculously I was instantly out of the shallow water and skimming along the surface of the river. The ride was bumpy since waves were created in the wake from the boat's engine. This was a minor detail to the thrill of this sport. I screamed in delight. I laughed with abandonment. My knuckles were white from holding tightly to the sturdy stick. Dan looked back at me from his position at the boat's steering wheel. His face was completely transfixed by his laughter. I was the first girl who had accepted his dare to try water skiing along the Monongahela. It was the summer between my freshman and sophomore year of study at The University. Some of the genes I inherited from my Mother gave me a love for adventure.

We continued at a great pace along the river for several miles. Cannot remember doing any other physical activity that gave me more of a high, not even a ride on a roller coaster at Kenny Wood Amusement

Park. Dan spotted a river steamboat in the distance. It was coming in our direction. Steamboats and water skiing are not safe mixtures in a river. Dan Lansdale was forced to make a wide turn to the opposite direction. The crude square platform on which I was perched did not have graceful curves with which to maneuver behind a powerboat. The simple wooden perch was suddenly jerked from beneath me as it encountered a large wave created from the turn. I was in the water in the middle of the Monongahela River but this did not produce fear. I knew how to swim and had experience with the river previously. Dan slowed the engine as he neared the spot where I was treading water. He was still grinning as he threw another rope toward me. I quickly grasped it. The motorboat was almost stationery at this point since Dan had pushed the throttle to the lowest position. "O, wow!" I said, breathlessly, as he leaned over the side of his boat to assist me in boarding the vessel. Soon we were speeding full force upstream against the northerly flow of the Monongahela far ahead of the approaching steamboat.

Steamboats were a regular sight along the river. They carried coal and other commodities from the mines along the riverbanks to Pittsburgh steel mills. There were regular stops along the way. Each mine had built trestles to the river. Coal was placed on small cars that looked like U shaped bathtubs. The cars ran along narrow gage tracks on top of the trestles from the mine to the river. At the river, a workman would release a lock support and literally tip the car to one side emptying its contents into a barge on the river. Then he would hook the small car to a pulley to take it back to the mine. When the barge was full it would be pushed by one of the steamboats downstream to Pittsburgh.

One of Dad's uncles worked on a steamboat. Uncle Bob made arrangements for Mom and me to go on board at one of the stops. Dad drove our old Model T Ford to pick us up as we disembarked several miles downstream at Roscoe, Pennsylvania. The steamboat intrigued me. It had a huge paddle wheel at the rear of the vessel. The paddle wheel was as tall as the boat. It was about three stories in height. The giant wheel provided the push to navigate the steamer. I loved holding the railing and watching the water cascade in various streams from the paddles on the wheel. The steamboat paddles were always painted red. A huge lever slid in and out of the hull of the boat. This motion of the lever governed the speed of the turning wheel. Energy was provided for the lever motion by a coal-fired furnace located in the lowest level of the steamboat. Uncle Bob took us on a tour of the boat. The heat of the furnace on the summer day visit made me appreciate the challenge the men faced as they manned the hot beast with kerchiefs tied around their necks to keep drops of perspiration from running down into the fabric of their shirts.

On the upper deck you could smell the smoke of the burning coal. The cook from the vessel's kitchen galley gave Mom and I lunch. It consisted of hot dogs served on folded slices of white bread and smothered with ketchup. We frequently sipped warm orange soda pop to wash our throats clear of the soggy red bread. In that era the steam boats did not have refrigerators.

The trip on the steamboat was delightful and unforgettable. For the first time I could see the river towns along the Monongahela from a totally new perspective. We also experienced the slow process of going through a lock. The steamboat captain reversed his engines several times and using the boat's rudder maneuvered into a large concrete box approximately 84 feet wide and 720 feet long. After we were in just the correct position a huge door closed behind us. The water slowly began to drain out of the box. I could sense the boat getting lower and lower in the box. In about thirty minutes another large door slowly opened in front of us. We were now at least five feet lower on the river. Behind us was the dam that held back the river. Its lock is still known as Lock 4 built 80 years ago.

The US Army Corp of Engineers maintains the lock and dam system. Dad's Uncle Bob Davis worked for fifty years on Lock 4. I remember Uncle Bob as being a happy person displaying frequent smiles. He was short and a bit stocky. Dad told me that Uncle Bob's physique was the result of his Welsh heritage. The river system consists of six locks and dams that run the length of the Monongahela. In 1783 the Virginia Assembly passed an ordinance for the clearing and extending of the navigation on this river. This was just seven years before Christian Lansdale (my fourth great maternal grandfather) purchased 200 acres of land along the Youghiogheny River. The Youghiogheny River and the Cheat River are tributaries that feed the Monongahela. Perhaps Christian Lansdale was aware of the legislative decree and surmised that the area had a good future. At that time in our country's history, rivers were a major part of transportation.

There are forty-six cities and towns along the
Monongahela River. My life is interwoven with
nineteen of the towns. Both my parents were born
near the river. They spent their entire lives in this
region of Pennsylvania. The Monongahela River has a
rich history associated with the westward expansion
of the nation during the colonial era and with the
development of America as an industrial power
beginning in the nineteenth century. My mother,
Elizabeth Lansdale, was born about a mile from
Brownsville. This river town produced the first
steamboat to make a full round-trip on the Mississippi
River. It was the same boat that General Andrew
Jackson commandeered in New Orleans to help defeat
the British.

Arthur Parker, a retired Executive Vice
President of the Waterways Association of Pittsburgh
has recently published a book about the
Monongahela. In his book Parker describes it as a
River of Dreams, A River of Sweat. Does that not also
describe many people's journey on earth? . . . .
dreams and sweat! . . . sweat and dreams!

The Lear Experience
"clearer insights"

Joe had one eye that faced to the left while the other eye was slightly tilted to the right. It was difficult to speak with him face to face because you did not know which eye was watching. His voice was sometimes raspy. His body usually clothed in faded blue jean trousers with matching shirt revealed a hard-working, lean, no nonsense farmer.

Joe Lear was the only son of the Lear family who lived at home. He was needed. Papa and Mama Lear were in the last stages of their lives. Both looked old and wizened to my eleven year old perspective. Mama Lear had legs that formed an upside down pear as she hobbled about the old farmhouse kitchen. Coffee was constantly brewing on the wood- burning stove. It gave the kitchen an aroma of a restaurant. A large jug of red wine was a regular part of the table setting. Papa Lear kept his small glass beside it. The old man would sit at the table drawing long and hard on his blackened pipe then let out small white puffs of smoke. Frequent sips of wine kept him happy and talkative.

The Lear's owned a farm across the highway from ours. The highway was the famous old toll road spanning the country from east to west known as US Route Forty. Mom and I would walk down the hill to the busy two lane historical road earlier used by people on horseback, stagecoaches and buckboard wagons. It was the only route in the early 1750's to the western part of our country. The Lear farmhouse was red brick and sat only about two car lengths from the busy highway. Lear's never used the front door. Mom and I would walk along the gravel pathway to the rear of the house.

A rugged trellis entwined by thick grape vines shaded the walkway to the back door. Lear's used the grapes to make their own wine. It was a tradition faithfully preserved from their homeland.

Both of the Senior Lear's spoke their own language, laced with Italian phrases, when they could not think of the correct English word. Papa Lear had worked and saved his money to buy passage to America. He purchased a farm in Pennsylvania. He then sent for his wife, Mama Lear. They had five children who were now adults. Four left the farm to marry and establish their own families. Son Joe was the exception. Perhaps his eye condition made him shy around young single women.

Mama and Papa Lear became grandparents to me, their eleven year old neighbor. My paternal grandparents were no longer living. Grandfather Winslow had died long before my parents married. Grandmother Winslow was totally deaf from an encounter with scarlet fever. It was difficult to speak with her. She was quite good at lip reading but you had to speak very slowly and always face her. Not being able to hear she would raise and lower her voice at odd times. This made me a little hesitant to get to close to her. She died of a stroke when I was in the first grade.

Mama and Papa Lear not only filled the role of grandparents to me. They became parents to my mother. She was an intriguing oddity to them, a divorced woman trying valiantly to run a dairy farm

alone. Papa Lear began selling bales of alfalfa to Mom
when we would run short of food for our fifty milk
cows. He would walk up the hill and offer tips to this
young divorcee. Papa Lear taught mother how to
make cheese. He even gave her some of the Lear
family starter to begin the fermentation. It was good
cheese with a mild slightly tangy flavor. The cheese
became a staple in our diets. Mama Lear would send a
loaf of freshly baked bread along with Papa Lear
when he visited the Winslow Farm to help their
"adopted" daughter and granddaughter during
harvest time the Lear's commanded their son Joe to
assist. Joe was already busy with the harvesting on the
Lear farm. He somehow managed to have enough
physical strength to help the Winslows up on the hill.
Papa and Mama Lear also sent their extended family
of borders to help.

Our friendship with Joe Lear grew. Mom knew
how to talk with Joe without being concerned with his
adverse eyes. After the dried hay was stacked away in
the barn, Joe, and two of the Lear borders would sit on
our back porch drinking cold milk. Happy, true to his
name, was the talkative one. He would tell stories

about his childhood spicing his performance with infectious laughter.

Many wonderful Sunday afternoons were spent at the Lear's. Mama Lear made delicious spaghetti. It was served with her homemade bread. I would quickly finish my portion. Papa Lear would pick up the large black pot from the stove and ladle another helping onto my plate. If I protested he would pause with the pot mid-air and shout, "Manja, Bambino, manja." This was translated "eat little girl." It was not hard to obey. Mom did not make spaghetti and Mama Lear's spaghetti was so yummy.

A motley collection of folks usually sat around the large kitchen table. They included Happy, Tojo, son Joe, Mama and Papa Lear and sometimes daughter Elizabeth from Charleroi. Elizabeth and Mom got along very well and would share long talks. I enjoyed watching the whole scene. It was wonderful to see many people around a table. It was also a nice change from eating with just Mom. In a way I missed my father but relished the tranquility of just the two of us.

Joe Lear was a faithful and helpful neighbor all during my early teen years. He became a fixture in my life. I never managed to settle on a comfortable way to look at him as he talked. Guess it was that as a young girl I was quite conscious of physical appearances. Mama Lear died when I was away attending college. Papa Lear became quite feeble and finally left the farm to live his remaining years with his daughter, Elizabeth in Charleroi. I never saw Mama and Papa Lear again.

While I was working on my master's degree in a nearby city, I would take the bus home to the farm. Mom had given up the daily milk delivery and was marketing the milk, in bulk, to a local farmer's cooperative. She had found several young boys to assist her morning and evening with farm chores. These young boys were part of a very large family who had purchased a lot on Joe Lear's farm. The parents were pleased that Mom needed their children's help. She gave generous donations to these kind neighbors.

Occasionally I would see Joe Lear walking along the highway. He had become a recluse. Eventually Joe sold the family farm to a successful dentist. The "gentleman farmer" reworked the old homestead. The farm became a showpiece, pasturing race horses. A distinctive sign was placed at the beginning of the driveway. It read: "Welcome to Tooth Acres."

Joe retained a small plot of his parent's farm. It was a portion very near our farm. He put up a single room shack constructed of recycled tin roofing and wood. He landscaped the small plot with an assortment of junk, parts of old cars, farm equipment, etc. It was truly an eyesore. It stood out vividly against the backdrop of the beautiful "Tooth Acres" and Mom's farm.

The last time that I saw Joe Lear was at my mother's funeral. Even though he had snow white hair and bore the usual signs of aging it was easy to recognize him. We chatted about times long ago. During our conversation I was overwhelmed by the radiant glow on Joe's face. His eyes were a light blue with deep circles of turquoise. Joe's eyes were embraced by love. I completely forgot the craziness of the distorted eyes that I once saw as a child. There is no doubt that sometime in his aloneness he had had a Divine Encounter. Joe Lear had been transformed. I also saw for the first time that he loved me as a father.

* * * * *

I missed the treasure in another person by focusing on physical appearance. When I listen and take another look at the individual my spirit is always rewarded. True friendship, I discovered, cannot be described with words and has no time limit. A parental figure gave me inspiration, not apparent at the time, but burst forth as a seed in later life.

Each person in this true story had a significant role. Little plus big formed an important whole. Remembering this part of my life makes me thankful for kindnesses these people showered on me. Life has greater meaning as I develop an appreciation of love not earned. To the extent I remember to sprinkle genuine niceties in the lives of others, joy overtakes me.

Conversation with Bob
"to be continued"

"Do you remember when you were my escort to the Rainbow Girl's Formal Dance?" I asked. "And do you remember that your brother, Paul, kicked you in the knees because you insisted on sitting in the back seat of the car as we were driving home?"

"I remember it as though it were yesterday," the 77-year-old man replied. His voice was strong on the phone. We both knew he was dying from advanced stage of cancer. He was in the intensive care unit at Sloane Kettering Hospital in New York. I knew he was grateful to recall memories of the past. It helped to soften the suffering of the hour.

Our conversation was cut short. A nurse and physician arrived at his bedside to work on another procedure. Two days later Bob uttered these words lying in his bed, "In the name of the Father, Son, and Holy Ghost." In the next second Bob's spirit departed. Paul, his only brother, who had kicked him so many years previously on a double date, stood at his bedside.

That was more than eighteen years ago. This is the first time I have had the emotional strength to write about my longtime friend, Bob Millhouse. He was my next-door farm neighbor. His parents owned the farm that adjoined my folks' property.

My first recollection of Bob Millhouse was seeing a tall lanky boy walking every day to school. He was six years my senior which is a significant number when you are 11-years-old. Every day I would walk to the intersection of rural route 88 and the famous route 40 which crossed the country. At this intersection I would board the Richeyville Bus and show my pass. Mom had purchased a special pass permitting me to use this service. The Centerville School System rules stated that if a student lived less than two miles from the school he/she could not use the bus. Mother believed it was a bit risky for me to walk along this busy highway. She did not have time to drive me daily to school since she was busy with managing our retail dairy business.

The Richeyville Bus was never able to keep to its schedule. Its appearance was in keeping with its erratic behavior. Unlike the other buses, it was a faded blue and white color in contrast to the normal orange and black. The bus had dents and rust spots in various places on its body.

Sometimes I would wait fifteen minutes, other times I would have to run with full speed to arrive at the intersection before the bus. I could see the rickety vehicle coming down one of the many hills along route 40. Occasionally, I would miss the bus and be forced to walk back home. This meant I would have to ask Mom to stop whatever project she was working on to get me to school without being late. They called late arrivals "tardy" in those days. The homeroom teacher would enter the number of late days each month on your report card. It was embarrassing.

Most days Bob would walk by my waiting spot carrying his books held together with a wide strap. He would smile, say hello, and keep on walking. I was eleven-years-old and very shy. It would have been painful if he had stopped to chat. I would not have known what to say. Several years later I learned that Bob and I shared a lot of ideas and concepts about living.

We both prided ourselves by thoroughly studying our school assignments. We enjoyed singing and were a part of our Methodist Fellowship Youth Choir. We also had a wild streak. We enjoyed doing what nobody would ever guess we would attempt.

One Halloween night, Bob, Kenneth Mallard (a young lad from a society family), and I joined Jimmy Wallace in his roadster for a trick or treating spree. We gathered a basket of rotten tomatoes from various fading fall gardens and proceeded to throw them on the front porches of every house in the area. One tomato that was not entirely rotten, but still hard like a soft ball, landed on the night light of a church member's porch. We heard broken glass falling to the wooden floor of the porch. Jimmy Wallace pressed the gas pedal to the floorboard of his roadster, speeding away as the rest of us howled in laughter. Why was that so much fun?

Bob loved to cook on the open grill. He and his brother, Paul, had built an elaborate outdoor room up the hill from their farmhouse. Our Methodist Youth Fellowship had many cookouts there. Bob loved to mix surprise ingredients in the ground beef to make the hamburgers compete with the best of today's gourmet cooks. He loved to create his own versions. He also mixed up a tasty crock of baked beans. His mother, Mrs. Millhouse, would compliment his fixings by creating a luscious bowl of potato salad. His Aunt Thelma, who lived on Millhouse farm, would bake a two layer cake smothered in icing. Our young people's group never lacked for food. We would eat, chat, and sing Jumonville camp songs in harmony. As the sky darkened and night arrived accompanied by many mosquitoes we would scatter to our homes.

Bob pursued his studies at the University of Pittsburgh after graduation from Centerville High. He rented a room near the campus but came home to his parent's farm every weekend. Bob and I would hold long serious discussions at the Methodist Youth Fellowship Meetings. He was like an older brother that I did not have. We would speak about our beliefs. Bob gave sermons at church for our Youth Day. They were always intellectual, a bit over most of the congregation's thought patterns. He decided to pursue further study at the prestigious Wharton Graduate School of Business at University of Pennsylvania in Philadelphia. During that time I took Bob's place as speaker on Youth Day at church.

I joined Kenneth Mallard (the young lad of a society family) at Penn State University. We were in the same class. Kenneth was a good friend of both Bob and Bob's younger brother, Paul. Paul and Kenneth Mallard were roommates at Penn State University until Kenneth joined a fraternity. Paul could not afford that luxury. Paul dated and then formed a serious "steady relationship" with my best friend, Ann Miller. Paul and Ann married as soon as he graduated from Penn State University. I was their Maid of Honor. Bob was the Best Man. Bob and I had maintained our friendship all those school years. We both enjoyed listening to classical music and solving the world's problems during deep thoughtful discussions.
It was Bob's suggestion to me that fostered a major turn in my life. He told me about the Graduate School

in Pittsburgh that prepared students to be executives in major department stores. That thought was refreshing to me. Nursing was not my calling. Being a Secretary had absolutely no appeal. A career in Teaching looked even more horrible to me. But being a "buyer in a department store"…now that was a glorious thought. I did enroll at the Graduate School after completing my degree at Penn State University. After graduation, I was offered an attractive position in Philadelphia at the then famous John Wanamaker Department Store.

I rented an apartment in center city Philadelphia near Rittenhouse Square. While attending Wharton in Philadelphia, Bob would take breaks from his studies, together, we would enjoy concerts, plays, and Philadelphia's many out of the spotlight restaurants that were undiscovered. One of our favorite haunts was the Gilded Cage. It was an avant-garde coffee house serving early versions of coffee blends like Starbucks. Young men and women would write poetry and read their writings aloud while sipping Espresso.

The Lord had plans for both Bob Miller's life and mine. Bob met and married the boss's daughter after he started work at Exxon's headquarters in New York City. I met an off-the-wall lad who has shared my life for many years.

Bob's wife, Ginny, is still living. They have three children and numerous grandchildren. This spring their only son married a nice Italian girl in a large wedding. Ginny sent us pictures. I could not believe my eyes. There was Bob in son Drew's smile, posture, and demeanor!

* * * * *

Bob is still my friend even though he left this world eight years ago. Someday our conversation will be continued uninterrupted. It is my observation that when old friends meet after being apart for many years, they take up exactly where they left off in their relationships. This phenomena is to me, a glimpse into eternity where time is not a factor. Yes, as human beings it is a difficult concept to grasp. Additional ideas to consider can be found in these intriguing references: Ecclesiastes 3:11, Isaiah 57:15 and Acts 15:18.

Neighbor who was a Stranger
"and yet a savior"

Lifting one slat of the Venetian blind on the window I could see the snowflakes swirling in the night wind. Spruce Street in center city Philadelphia was covered in about four inches of snow. Cars pass by occasionally with speed considerably slower than usual. Dad had called from the airport about thirty minutes earlier to tell me his plane had landed safely after a two-hour delay. He said he was going to get a cab and would see me within the hour.

My Father had left Mom in charge of the family farm in order to spend two days in the big city helping his only child celebrate her birthday. It was a rare occasion for both parents to visit at the same time since the fifty dairy cows, numerous calves, and year old heifers needed morning and evening attention. Aunt Margaret and Uncle Hub were going to help with the milking chores.

A fierce January snowstorm was hovering over the Philadelphia area and had given me a good excuse to worry. Sometimes planes crashed while trying to land in heavy snowfall. It was always difficult to get taxis when the weather was not perfect. Dad was an impatient person and often became frustrated with delays and other various challenges. Would he arrive in a grumpy mood?

As I was watching the snowflakes, a taxi turned the corner and unto Spruce Street. I waited, breathing short shallow anxious breaths. Sure enough the cab slowed to a stop in front of my brownstone apartment. A familiar silhouette emerged from the vehicle. I was so excited and relieved.

My apartment was on the first floor of an old brownstone mansion. It was an efficiency apartment but appeared larger because the room had fifteen-foot high ceilings. The two windows faced the street. They were ten feet high with elegant wooden shutters that recessed into side openings. The room itself was spacious. At one end was a wall with French doors that concealed a sink, small stove, and refrigerator. Since the sink was mounted on the wall with no cupboard below, I had purchased a rolling table that provided a miniscule workspace for meal preparation, and a shelf below for the necessary skillet and one cooking pan. To make the apartment cozy I had purchased an antique sewing machine from the buyer at John Wanamaker Department Store where I worked. She had taken the old relic in on a trade for the purchase a new Singer. I explained that my budget was meager so she gave me the machine at a good price. It, too, was a Singer. It was so old that the only function was sewing a straight stitch. But it was sturdy and proved to be more than adequate equipment for me to create a slipcover for my day bed, pillows for my circle chair, and drapes that pulled across the efficiency kitchen. The entire apartment was quite attractive. I had splurged on the fabric. It was an elegant stripe pattern of blue, green, and crème. I was proud of my work that had taken several weekends to complete. I could hardly wait to show Dad my creative talent.

It was about ten thirty in the evening when Dad finished paying the cab fare and walked up the steps of the stately brown stone. I had arrived home about seven. My day at Wanamaker's had been a taxing one. I took the streetcar marked "Spruce Street" and leaned my head on the window while it rambled along slowly. Streetcars did not do well in snow. Cars would get in front of the trolley causing it to screech to a stop. The conductor would wait for a few minutes then pull a rope which produced a "clang clang" sound hoping to clear the traffic. The car drivers totally ignored the "clang clang". We would have to simply sit there until the path became clear again. By the time I signaled my stop to the conductor, it was already ten minutes after the hour of six. I decided to treat my weary body to one of the fabulous sandwiches at Day's Deli. I added a bowl of their fresh home- made soup. What a delectable respite, sitting in one of the warm booths, watching the snow descend outside the window while the spoonfuls of hot vegetables renewed my strength.

I felt so much better as I walked the several city blocks to my apartment. Since Dad was expected at about eight, I decided to take a hot shower and put on my comfy pajamas. I wanted to be bright eyed and filled with enthusiasm to welcome my father. As Dad was climbing the brownstone stoop stairs, I flung open my apartment door, ran into the hallway, and scurried to the outer door to open it for him. Wanting to be modestly attired, I grabbed my full-length fur coat from the coat rack and pulled it on over my pajamas.

As Dad stepped into the hall, he placed his suitcase on the floor in order to give me a hug. It was then I heard the door to my apartment close with a thud. It took a minute or two to realize the enormity of the situation that Dad and I now faced. Here I stood in fur coat and slippers. I had no key to the apartment. It was now nearly eleven thirty on a stormy evening. I did not know any of the other people who rented apartments in the brown stone mansion. I did not even know how many units the building contained. There was one other door on the first floor. I knocked on it but there was no response. Dad commented that we might have to go to a hotel but how would we get there? Cabs did not travel on a regular basis down Spruce Street.

I walked up half a flight of stairs and pounded on the door of the next apartment. There was no answer. The halls were dimly lit and I did not want to climb any more stairs. Desperately, I continued to pound on the door. Finally, after about five minutes a muffled man's voice called from inside the door. "What do you want?" he asked.

"I live on the first floor," I explained. "I went into the hall to open the front door for my father and my door slammed shut locking me out."

"Well, I can't help you. I do not have any keys for your apartment."

"But would you call our landlord for me? If you can get an answer, tell him I will take a cab to his place to get another key. Then I also need you to call the cab. Explain to our landlord that I am desperate."

There was a long agonizing pause. "Well, I will try. I'm sure he will be upset about getting a phone call so late."

"I know," I replied, feeling afraid and foolish. A long period of time passed. Dad waited on the first floor. He, too, was worried. I stood there on the upper landing in my slippers, pajamas, and fur coat. My heart was pounding and my palms were sweaty.

The door did not open but I heard the same muffled voice say that he had talked to the landlord and also ordered a cab.

"Oh, thank you so much," I said.

"Okay, Okay," he said gruffly.

I padded down the stairs to the first floor. Dad and I waited in the hallway for the cab. The snow was still falling and the wind was swirling the flakes in dervish like dances. One half hour later the cab pulled up in front of the brown stone. Dad toted his suitcase along. With this crazy daughter, one never knew what might happen next. I felt the cold wet snow surround my flimsy slippers. It was like walking in my bare feet. My toes became very cold in just the short distance from the front stoop to the cab.

The landlord was about ten city blocks from the brownstone mansion. No caretaker lived at the mansion. We told the cab to wait while I slipped and slopped across the street in my now soggy slippers. The landlord immediately opened the door when I knocked and handed me the key. I thanked him with passion. He did not say a word.

On the return cab ride to the brownstone I told Dad that it was a good thing that he had cash for the fare and that I had at least put on my fur coat over my pajamas.

All Dad could say was, "Boy Oh Boy, I thought we were in for it. Couldn't imagine how we were going to get out of this mess!"

Feeling quite sheepish I managed, "I am so thankful that the man whose apartment is at the first landing finally answered!"

The two of us were exhausted as we entered my apartment. Neither said a word. I pulled out the camp bed for Dad to sleep on. In less than ten minutes he was curled up on the cot with Grandma's handmade quilt pulled up around his chin.

The last thing he said before falling asleep was, "We came very close to sitting on the floor in the hallway all night."

"That's for sure," I muttered, as I turned out the lights and snuggled under the covers of my day bed rubbing my stiff cold feet together.

To this day I do not know the name of the neighbor, nor to my knowledge ever saw his face. But I will be forever grateful that he <u>did</u> respond to the knocking of a desperate young woman on a stormy night in January. Some truths remain the same over the centuries. Check Luke 18:1-4 in your Bible.

* * * *

All the old mansions on Spruce Street have now been purchased by wealthy baby boomers wanting a life in the city. One by one the mansions have been restored to elegant private homes. It is nice to know that someone is still enjoying the fifteen-foot ceilings on the first floor and looking out the tall windows with wooden shutters. The bones of the old mansions were regal. I can imagine the grandeur of each home. Was told the mansions are selling for over a million in restored state. What stories the old brownstones could tell if they could speak!

Shopping in Third Dimension
"dating adventures"
Part One Beginning Saga

Have you ever heard of an arranged marriage? It happens when someone with authority selects a suitable bride or groom for a person under his or her care. The practice is a common thing in most of Africa and The Middle East today. It was certainly common in Biblical times. But not in the United States! Dating and courtship are so popular there are even TV shows devoted to the game. Strange as it may seem, my marriage to David is an arranged marriage.

My first date was at age sixteen, a limit imposed by wise parents. However, in first grade I was greatly taken in a boy named Lee McCormick. I looked forward to school each day just to be in the class with him. He was a bright student. So I made an effort to match his grades. At the age of six, I thought that was the way to win a boy's heart. I soon learned that did not work. But it was nice to get strokes from my parents on good report cards so I focused in that area.

Later in the Methodist Youth Fellowship, I met and became madly infatuated with Kerry Mound. My stomach would get a funny feeling every time I saw him. Kerry and I had several classes in high school together. Our history teacher was an elderly spinster who had many years of teaching experience. She taught my mother's history class. By the time she tried to instill a love of history in me she faced a formidable task. She dyed her hair a brilliant carrot red. She was a bit hard of hearing but still had sharp eyes. For some reason I always felt an urge to laugh in each of her classes. She told the same stories she had recited to my mother years before. Mother and I would compare notes and laugh with deep belly laughs at home. The teacher's name was Anna Mae Hargrave. Miss Hargrave also taught Kerry's father. He and his father compared stories, too. The two of us could guess what would be said about the Battle of Antietam, etc. Kerry would look across the aisle, hold his history text in front of his nose, then make funny faces. To maintain composure I would quickly busy myself with notebook writing to ward off a burst of laughter. Sometimes it did not work and a giggle would escape from my throat. Miss Anna Mae would whirl around to see who was responsible. Strangely, she tolerated both Kerry and I. Perhaps she was remembering our parents as students. Kerry and I were friends. We pulled many mischievous stunts in class and at the Methodist Youth Fellowship. But one day I learned the tough lesson that a friend was not necessarily a date. Kerry asked another member of the youth group to the prom. It was my first dead end in the dating game.

Moving on from the Kerry lesson I dated Nick who was the class president and captain of the football team. This time my parents did not approve. Nick and I would find ways to have dates in combination with school activities. This avoided confrontation with Mom and Dad. Nick's ancestors came from Czechoslovakia. My parents were Anglo Saxons. They warned that only trouble would follow from this courtship. Marriage would not work between British and Eastern European cultures. I told Nick about my parent's attitude. He somehow accepted it. Nick joined the Marines after High School. I left our community to attend Penn State University.

Part Two
"sanding rough edges"

As a freshman at The University, I found myself in a company of college women with an unusual advantage. The ratio of men to women was twelve to one. The officials had decided to allow freshmen women to live on the main campus in central Pennsylvania for the first time in the school's history. It was even more favorable in my curriculum. I was one of only two women in the College of Business Administration. The other women students were in The Colleges of Home Economics, Commercial, and Education. My classes were statistics, marketing, accounting, economics, principles of management etc. The potential for getting a date was like standing under a tree loaded with fruit on the branches as well as the ground. Having been taught to make the best of life's circumstances, I wasted no time to put that theory into action.

It was early morning, a weekday, a time when serious students should have been focusing on studies. I sat at my desk thinking about my high school advisor's parting comments at graduation. "Oceola, when you begin your college experience, remember that you must get involved with extra-curricular activities. You have been so focused on academics here at Centerville High School that you are in danger of becoming lopsided in your personality. There is more to life than study. Have some fun. This will help you get a good position when you graduate. Employers look for well-rounded candidates."

While these words bounced about in my mind, the phone rang. Donald Swanson was calling to see if I would be interested in attending a movie matinee with him as an impromptu experience. I enjoyed doing impromptu things. It was like an adventure. Donald Swanson was a senior at The University with nearly all of his graduation credits completed. He was a nice young man. He was President of his Fraternity and also President of an Academic Society. His major was entomology, the study of bugs. I was not impressed with bug study, but Donald was a person who brought enjoyment to those around him. I quickly agreed to join him for the movie.

A few minutes after Donald's call, I received another call for a date the very same day. This was from Fred Nelson. He, too, was a fine young man. He was a member of the ROTC and looked handsome in the uniform. His major was atomic engineering, a field of study I felt was cutting edge. Fred was also a senior at The University with most of his required courses completed. The classes he attended at this point were electives, fun and easy. This gave him more time for socializing.

Remember the twelve to one ratio of men to women on campus? I reminded myself of the high school counselor's advice to have fun. The counselor was obviously referring to activity in campus groups, but I focused only on the fun aspect. When you are selecting fruit fallen at your feet from a laden tree, each one looks delicious.

A quick decision was made in my mind. I said to Fred on the phone, "I am busy this afternoon, but I could manage to have dinner with you tonight." Fred was enthusiastic about the idea. All was set. The rest of the day was laced with great anticipation. Frankly I liked both young men.

Donald Swanson arrived promptly and we strolled down The University's Old Main Promenade lined with magnificent oak trees. Donald and I attended the movie, an old classic film in black and white, thoroughly enjoying it. The theatre was filled with college students who munched popcorn and felt free to shout comments at the screen. Donald and I joined them enthusiastically. You might call this activity group psychology. It provided an emotional outlet for many of the students.

After the movie Donald asked me if I would like to have a milkshake at the Dutch Pantry, a popular student hangout. I informed him that as much as I would like to do this, I simply had to get back to the dormitory. After all it was a weekday! We chatted and laughed along the walk back to the dorm. Donald had a delightful personality and made friends quickly. The only possible negative about him was his selection of academic pursuits. What person would be interested in spending time fiddling with bugs, dead or alive?

Donald and I arrived back at the dorm in a timely manner. I had just about fifteen minutes to spend before Fred Nelson would arrive to escort me to dinner. Fred was definitely the dinner date type of gentleman. He was smooth in mannerisms, polished in conversation, maintained the hint of a smile in his eyes, and focused on the other person as he listened.

I said goodbye to Donald in the dorm lounge and entered the powder room on the first floor of the dorm. I made a quick mirror check. Satisfied that I looked presentable I walked leisurely back to the dorm lounge to meet Fred. He had arrived promptly and rose from his chair with an engaging smile to greet me. It was at that moment I spotted Donald Swanson across the lobby talking to the dorm's housemother, Mrs. McCracken. Donald with his friendly ways had won the heart of this gray haired grandmother type of dorm overseer. She and Donald were chatting and laughing. Almost at the same time that I saw Donald, he saw me. The look on Donald's face is one I shall never forget. He realized that I was now going out on a date with another young man. I wanted to completely vanish but miracles like that never happen, even when the situation is desperate, never mind that I had created the humiliating problem without any assistance.

As Fred and I walked out the front door, he asked me why that fellow talking to the housemother was looking at me so intently. I told Fred that Donald was a friend. "You should have introduced me," Fred stated. We walked silently the rest of the way to Lyon's Corner House for dinner. Fred appeared to be in deep thought. I was too embarrassed to think of good conversation. My stomach felt like I had just had swallowed a bowl full of cherry pits.

That day's experience taught me several lessons. I was ashamed of my self-centeredness. I realized that I had much to learn in personal relationships. I was an only child and thought it normal to be the center of attention for better or worse. My parents were strict and insisted I obey totally without any objections. Living on a dairy farm with fifty cows to milk night and morning presented me with many chores to keep busy. However, cows were not people. With no brothers or sisters to jostle with, I focused on the many duties associated with farm living.

School friends were sparse. I listened intently to the teacher of each class. I always carefully fulfilled each homework assignment. All of my grades were 'A' or better. I often thought of the day I brought home my first report card. The teacher had written across it, "*Second on the honor roll.*" The first comment my parents made was "Why weren't you first?" Ashamed and hurt I determined to be first on the school's honor roll for the rest my school experiences. I succeeded.

My parents also taught me high moral codes of conduct. This added to my shame in this faux-paux situation. How totally self-absorbed and thoughtless I had been. The act of accepting two dates in one day with two wonderful young men revealed some of my wild impetuous nature. I had no choice but to confess to Donald and Fred what I had done. Much to their credit, when I confessed my actions, both men forgave me. Donald Swanson later presented me with his Fraternity Pin and sent me fresh bouquets of flowers each week. The flowers always arrived at the desk in the dorm lounge with an attached envelope addressed to Oceola Winslow. The news soon spread around the building. I was the envy of all the residents. Donald Swanson graduated from Penn State University at the end of my freshman year. He went to California to pursue a master's degree in entomology. Letters did not replace the personal interaction. We drifted apart

He later told me on the phone that he had met a girl "just like me" and was now engaged. Thankfully, Donald graciously overlooked my faults when making this statement.

Fred Nelson graduated the same year and began his career with Westinghouse Atomic Sub Division in Pittsburgh. Phone calls, letters, and frequent visits kept our friendship growing. Fred remained part of the Army Reserve. He was given an assignment on the Island of Oahu as part of his reserve training. During my senior year Fred asked me to come to Hawaii over the Christmas break. I was chaperoned by my dear Mother. While visiting Fred in Hawaii, I was given a lovely emerald cut diamond engagement ring. I was engaged and in love.

There were a few flaws in the relationship. He was Catholic. I was Protestant. He agreed to be married in my church and that our children would not need to be Catholic. However, shortly before the marriage a Rosary fell out of his pocket as he removed his coat. I began to realize he was very devout. So was I. This fact could cause problems.

Shortly another flaw became evident.
Wedding plans were well developed including the
invitations. Meanwhile, as a very independent
woman, I announced to Fred that I had applied and
been accepted in the Graduate School of Business at
the University of Pittsburgh. Although Fred had now
returned to his job at Westinghouse in Pittsburgh, he
was truly upset about my new pursuit. Fred had plans
for being married to a "full time homemaker". He
informed me that he was already earning a salary
sufficient to support a wife and children. We sadly
postponed the wedding. I returned the engagement
ring. We continued to date but our infrequent times
together were strained. Fred found a devout Catholic
woman who was delighted to simply be his wife.

Part Three
"blind trust"

I attended Graduate School at the University,
receiving honors. Meanwhile I continued the process
of dating but in a more subdued manner. Each man
became a good friend but not a candidate for long
term marriage commitment. None of the gentlemen
friends were a good match my adventurous self,
mixed with many short comings.

By this time I had begun my career as a buyer
for John Wanamaker Department Store. The work was
exciting but evenings in my lovely brown stone
apartment in center city Philadelphia were very
lonely. I began attending the young people's socials at
Tenth Presbyterian Church and dated several nice
fellows but they could not compare to Fred.

Finally, one evening I knelt beside my bed. "Oh God, I said, "you know how lonely I feel. I would like to have a husband. You also know things have not been successful in the dating game. Now I am asking you to send me a husband. YOU select him. I will marry the man you choose."

God did not delay long. Within a short time a tall young man with dark curly hair came up to me at one of the church socials. "Are you one of the nurses?" he asked. "No, I'm in retailing," was my cool reply. "I am with Snellenburgs." It was a competitor. We chatted shop talk for a while. "It's raining, would you like a ride home?" he asked. Well why not, I thought. As I slide into his car I spotted a set of baby booties swinging from the rear view mirror. How uncouth of him! Here I was with a married man. On the drive to my apartment I managed to ask how many children he had. "Oh those are MY baby shoes." he said flatly. What a strange person he is, I thought.

As he walked me to the door he pulled out his little black book and requested my phone number. Why I would ever give it to him is a mystery except for the Holy Spirit. You see this was the man God selected for me to marry. We dated for about three months. He asked me if I knew how to cook eggs. What a nut I thought. I did not know it was a test. He wanted to see if I could prepare them as well as his mother. I passed.

We would often go out with another couple. The fellow was David's best friend. The two of them had a sense of humor that was so dry it floated far above my head. We girls would go to the powder room during the evening and compare notes on how weird the guys were.

One evening the strange David asked me to marry him. I found myself saying yes. Again it had to be the work of the Holy Spirit. I was certainly NOT in love with him and I thought he was unusual. But my inner spirit believed that God had sent him, so with a great leap of faith we were married.

God never makes a mistake. He honored my inner spirit's trust. He blessed me with an absolutely wonderful husband. He is my best friend. I have since learned to grasp his dry sense of humor. David is also the brother I never had. He is a partner in adventure. He is an excellent listener. He is kind and considerate. His love has helped me understand the Love of God. Somewhere along the way I have fallen deeply in love with the man of my arranged marriage. This love is lasting, fulfilling, and has stood the test of the years.

How I thank God for presenting me with such a delightful partner.

* * * * *

The entire experience of shopping in the third
dimension from first grade to well beyond the
establishment of my career enabled me to see myself
in an honest light. Once a person can name and accept
revealed faults, he or she become free to be the person
God created them to be. I learned that true wisdom is
a gift. It cannot be earned but can be acquired with an
open mind and spirit. I personally became aware of a
basic truth for my life. Unlike humans who sometimes
try to control us, the Creator waits for us to seek Him.

Kip
"early life"

Kip rubbed his leg. It hurt. The straw he had
stuffed into his mattress bag had separated during the
night leaving his leg to rest on the unbending wooden
floor. He sighed long and deep an watched the cold of
the loft transform his breath into a pearly white mist.
He could hear his mother making coffee. He did not
need to get dressed. He had slept in his clothes to
endure the cold. He had just two pair of trousers and
two shirts. His coat was one that had been worn by his
older brother. There were no mittens of gloves. Kips
single pair of shoes listed to one side. His two older
brothers had already worn the soles along the edge by
their walking style.

Every day Kip and his sister, Martha walked to
the one room school. He was always eager to carry the
two-tiered pail that held lunch for he and his sister
especially on winter mornings. The bottom had two
slices of bread, the top hot coffee. The heat felt good
on his bare fingers. There was no breakfast. The
children were grateful for the bread they would enjoy
at lunch. The coffee had canned milk in it giving the
beverage a sweet flavor. They would sit together and
dip the bread into the coffee. Neither would talk
much. There was little talking at home. Kip and
Martha could not speak with their mother, Agnes. She
had an encounter with typhoid fever. The disease left
the children's mother totally deaf. She rarely saw their
tears and never heard their voices.

Sometimes Kip was pleased that his Mom
could not hear. That meant she was spared listening to
the loud cries from his father. Kip would shudder

when he remembered the day the men carried his father to their two-room rented home from the mine. The wheels of a run-away coal car had mangled his father's legs and injured his back. There was no money for pain pills, no wheel chair. There was no welfare, no Medicaid. The year was 1910. Kip's Dad was bedridden. Every movement made him scream. He could not use his legs. Arthritis quickly appeared in the lower back and twisted leg bones. Older brother John took care of their Dad at night and weekends after school. He was the strongest and could lift his helpless Father. The home had no electricity, no running water. It was heated by a single cooking stove.

After the mining accident, the family had to focus all efforts just to get enough food to eat. Kip knew there was no money to save to buy a home of their own. His deaf mother, Agnes, took in washings from the kindly neighbor's in exchange for flour and other staples. The washing machine was a large tub with a scrub board. Water had to be carried from the spring near the little barn. It was then heated on the cooking stove.

Kip's Grandpa lived with his family. Luckily Grandpa owned a horse. In the summer kip and Grandpa would plow the fields for planting by hand. Half of the crops would go to the landlord in exchange for rent. Kip was thankful that there was still food left. He would help his mother can the vegetables and smoke the meat from their pig for the long winter in Western Pennsylvania. Kip and his mother devised ways to communicate with their hands. If Kip spoke very slowly looking directly at her she could grasp some of the things he said. Many times her guess would be far afield He would turn away so she could not see his eyes brimming with tears.

Two years after the mining accident, Kip's father died from pneumonia. His oldest brother, John, stopped school to enter the mine. His oldest sister was sent to his mother's parent's home in the nearby town. This was one less person to feed and clothe. Grandpa and Kip continued to till the land together. Kip was able to finish the eighth grade. Then his father's brother found the thirteen-year-old boy a job on at the local railroad round house. It was the repair station for the railroad engines. The round house was across the Monongahela River. Every day Kip would walk several miles to the little shack at the edge of the river. He would jump into the little boat called a skiff. The boat's owner would row across the river. Kip paid him a nickel. Kip continued working at the round house for forty-six years; most of those years Kip had a garden. It was like the one he and Grandpa planted on the tiny rented farm years earlier.

Kip
Part two
"after retirement"

In the forty-six year time span that Kip worked for the railroad many changes occurred. The round house was closed. The steam engines no longer powered trains. They were replaced by diesels. The steel industry and consequently the coal mines lost profitability. All the river towns became forlorn. Younger residents moved elsewhere to find employment. Kip moved to the metropolitan area of the Twin Cities in Minnesota. He was now known as Clifford. He matured well with a thick head of grey-white hair. His wardrobe reflected the nuances of urban attire.

Clifford discovered a way to make friends. He discovered how to introduce himself to newcomers in the neighborhood. He discovered a way to build a reputation. He discovered the secret to getting job offers without interviews. How?

Clifford developed the art of creating and baking fabulous pies. Cliff was a shy person who knew how to endear himself to others once he had managed to hurdle the initial contact. A delicious piece of pie presented to a new neighbor down the hall provided exactly the right tool for this endeavor. He would knock gently on their door. When the apartment's occupant peered through the safety hole they would see a clean cut, modestly dressed yet distinguished looking gentleman with wavy grey hair, holding a plate laden with a generous slice of pie.

Clifford would hold out the plate and say, "I just finished baking a pie and thought you might enjoy it with a cup of coffee." Cliff's pies not only looked good, every morsel of the creation gave the mouth an exquisite delight of flavor and texture. Using variations of this approach Clifford quickly established his reputation. He was the pie man of Calvary Complex. Residents began talking to their friends about Cliff's pies. Soon he was well known around Golden Valley.

Clifford worked part time as a special assistant to the owner of a local jewelry manufacturer. He would take a piece of pie to any person having a birthday at the plant. His fame spread throughout the organization. A friend of Cliff's boss offered him a job baking pies for his classy restaurant. Cliff refused citing that he was retired and pie baking was a hobby that gave him great rewards.

Clifford's success was due in part to his creative imagination. He would experiment with various combinations of ingredients. One afternoon he assembled a fruit pie consisting of green grapes too sour to eat and fresh blueberries While in the oven the unorthodox combo produced so much juice it overflowed the crust and covered the bottom of the oven producing a billow of pungent smoke. Cliff's apartment fire alarm responded promptly. Bells sounded on every floor of the high rise. The Golden Valley Fire Department located just across the street dispatched one of its huge trucks accompanied with a dozen ready to act men. Meanwhile Cliff had pulled the pie out of the oven and opened all windows. He then called the front desk to inform them what had happened.

The disgruntled firemen soon began to get a new perspective on the situation. Yes the incident was sparked by one of the old men who lived in the center. But the piece of grape and blueberry pie each man was given tasted so unique and delicious they departed smiling.

That evening in the community dining room the other residents shouted out as Cliff entered the room. "Here comes the man who brought about all the commotions this afternoon." The shy 75-year-old man held his body erect and shouted back, "Bet you wished you could get all that attention. Besides I was simply perfecting a new pie to offer as a gift on each person's birthday" Things settled. But Clifford was shrewd enough to order several gadgets in a novelty cooking catalogue to avoid future engagements with the fire department across the street.

******

At eighty-years-old, Cliff {Kip} planted his last garden. He would hoe a row for a while then sit on the grass to rest. He was on kidney dialysis. He had little strength. At the end of the garden work, Cliff took several large tomatoes from the vines, got in his car and drove to his daughter's home. He sat in a comfortable chair, leaned back and looked out the window. "It won't be long now. Soon I shall be able to sit and talk to Mom and Dad like I always wanted to do."

******

A few weeks later the Jewelmont Corporation hired a bus to carry their employees to the Kip`'s memorial service. Kip had spent twelve years of his retirement working part time for this company. One by one those who had worked with Kip shared with his daughter the delightful experience they had working with him. He had listened to their cares, and made them laugh. Kip, acquainted with poverty and suffering at an early age had truly made a difference in many people's lives. Kip was my father.

My boat is small
Your sea so vast
Dear Lord
protect me

Betty in my Heart
"treasures inherited"

"She looks like a young bride" a neighbor commented as she viewed my mother's body lying in the coffin. It was easy to understand the observation. Betty Winslow was dressed in my white lace pantsuit. I had worn it to a dance in Portugal. Somehow it seemed right to select that outfit. The dressy lace ensemble could have easily been featured on the pages of Vogue. I had purchased it in Dayton's oval room. It was during my "fashion conscious" phase. I liked to wear the most daring new creations of the moment. I had had so much fun wearing it that night in Lisbon. David and I were attending a concert featuring "fada". Fada is part of the cultural music in Portugal. The songs are written and sung with longing of unrequited love themes. In the middle of the program, the performer left the stage and asked me to dance with him. He was obviously taken by the white lace outfit. It DID stand out in the crowd.

Mom was always a tiny feminine looking woman. She was barely five feet three inches tall and weighed only 120 pounds. Her figure was the silent envy of many in her circle of friends. At my father's retirement party, his work buddies took him aside and asked him what it was like to be married to such a young woman! Her hair had only a few white strands sprinkled among the shoulder length tresses. Her face had no wrinkles in spite of the battering of 67 years on earth.

My choice of the white lace pantsuit with flared, ruffled trousers was based more on the persona of Betty than her youthful appearance. Many of the nurses at the hospital where Mom died thought she was my sister. Of course that made me realize I must have looked old for my age. To simply focus on the appearance of my mother would make you miss the true value of this daughter of God.

Betty did not think of any limitations. Being a woman was no handicap for her. She simply did men's work in her own firm manner. She had an uncanny sense of how mechanical things functioned. Not only did she repair our farm equipment, but to her credit, neighboring male farmers would ask Betty to "take a look at their malfunctioning equipment." I do not ever recall a time that she was not successful in completing the repair.

Betty believed totally in good work ethics. She placed a sign in our dairy "*Success Comes by Keeping On After Everyone Else Quits.*" As my mother, she forbade me to do two things:

1. Say no to anything she told me to do...after all she was the parent, I the child.
2. Say "I can't"...she would emphatically declare to me "There is no such thing as can't, it means you won't. Keep trying until you master the challenge.

Mom was a perfect role model. I never heard her say "I can't." Sometimes I would overhear my father say to his friends. "Betty can do anything. I have never seen her stumped. She could just do ANYTHING." She was a good public speaker, always presenting a positive message. She made lovely clothes on her Singer machine. She learned to ride a bicycle in her late forties. She was daring in the decoration of our farmhouse. Walls were painted a deep rich fuchsia color complemented by stark white woodwork at the fireplaces, bay windows, and other architectural features of the farmhouse. She dug up a large birch tree that was growing on an aging slate dump. Slate dump, for those who did not live in Southwestern Pennsylvania, is the residue that was piled at the entrance of coal-mines after the mineral was extracted. This tree decorated with artificial but realistic looking birds and a real nest was a focal point placed near our open winding staircase.

Betty won several ribbons from the State of Pennsylvania for the quality of milk produced at Winslow's Dairy. She concocted her own mixture of grains to grind for the dairy cows making certain they were well nourished. She designed our dairy's signature container for retail milk delivery. It was a half-gallon size with green lettering and featured a golden cow's head to represent our Guernsey herd. Our motto printed on each bottle read *"America's Finest Table Milk."* Indeed, our reputation for quality milk was well known among the local doctors. If a new born infant could not digest its own mother's breast milk, the doctor would suggest Winslow's Guernsey Dairy's milk as a substitute.

She worked diligently beginning at five in the morning until eight or nine at night. She was the first woman I ever saw wearing jeans with no fly front. The other farm women would pull on men's trousers because there were no ladies' jeans at that time. Betty believed the Biblical injunction that a woman should not wear men's clothing. She simply sat down at her Singer sewing machine and cleverly removed the fly front. She purchased a size larger than she needed which enabled her to totally disguise the transformation. She wore ladies' blouses with the jeans. When working out in the field beneath the searing heat of summer sun, Betty wore a small white boy's cap. I still have one of her caps in my box of treasures.

You could not say that all work was Betty's life. She managed to teach Sunday school to high school girls giving white Bibles to those who memorized selected verses. Under Betty's tutelage very few missed getting a Bible! She took trumpet lessons and loved to play hymns. The trumpet was her favorite musical instrument because this instrument is mentioned in the Bible as heralding the return of Christ. Mom's obvious favorite passage in Holy Scripture was the 13th chapter of Corinthians on God's definition of genuine love. Mom had a tender heart that was easily wounded but she never retaliated or spoke ill of the offending individual. She would simply pray for that person.

Mom was an excellent cook, using great imagination in combining ingredients. She could rustle up a meal from one of her canned jars lined neatly in the cool basement or she would dig up root vegetables left in the ground after fall harvest. Her pies were outstanding. She rarely fried foods. Her forte was oven baked dishes. They could be roasting or baking while she did other household chores. My father loved her pies and with the help of a no fail crust recipe from his sister carried on the tradition of pies par excellence after Mom entered her true home for eternity.

Betty loved to do new things. She learned to roller skate at age 65. She enjoyed being the program chairperson at Grange and dreamed up many creative presentations.

Mom was faithful in letter writing. I could count on receiving at least one letter each week when we lived in Minnesota while my parents resided in Pennsylvania. Each letter always exhorted me to put Jesus first since He was the only important part of anyone's life.

Betty had an off-beat sense of humor. Her laughter was deep and hearty. One time she and I were spending a late night at the movies. A particular scene tickled her funny bone and she began to laugh. Now that scene was not supposed to be funny. No other person in the audience was laughing, but with her infectious and genuine enjoyment soon the entire theatre was filled with laughter. The theater manager entered the auditorium to determine the cause. As a teenage girl I was embarrassed. I kept saying, "Sh...Sh" to her but this only made every person laugh even more. I must confess that I have inherited this off-beat sense of humor and rather enjoy being an *"odd person."*

Mom has been enjoying her true home for nearly fifty three years. Her garments are far more glorious than the earthly white lace outfit that covered her empty body lying in the coffin. Betty IS now a young bride...she will never age, she will always be part of Christ's body, His bride. I truly look forward to the time I can join her along with all family and friends who have crossed the Jordon. But meanwhile I shall live my own life to the fullest with the grace of

God, and thank Him for giving me some of Betty's genes.

* * * * *

When I became an adult, my Mother began to share some of the sad experiences of her life.

As my mother she modeled for me a living example of positive thinking.

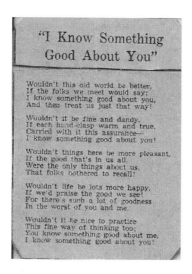

"I Know Something Good About You"

Wouldn't this old world be better,
If the folks we meet would say:
I know something good about you,
And then treat us just that way!

Wouldn't it be fine and dandy,
If each hand-clasp warm and true,
Carried with it this assurance—
I know something good about you!

Wouldn't things here be more pleasant,
If the good that's in us all,
Were the only things about us,
That folks bothered to recall!

Wouldn't life be lots more happy,
If we'd praise the good we see!
For there's such a lot of goodness
In the worst of you and me.

Wouldn't it be nice to practice
This fine way of thinking too;
You know something good about me,
I know something good about you!

I learned a truth for myself simply by growing up under her parenting. She had no illusions concerning her skills as a mother. She would remind me [when I was an adult] that nearly every parent "does the best they know how." As human beings most of us try to do the right things. Sometimes we need to read or listen to other sources. Over three thousand years ago a wise king wrote a truth worth noting. You can find it in Proverbs 24:6.

Three Women
"three beacons"

Although God gave each of us a unique set of genes that determine what we become, He graciously gave us the gift of making choices. This is a powerful tool. We can influence the genes of our DNA by our thoughts, choices, and role models. The combination of the written word, movies, and television has enabled me to select women that I admire. They are:

1. Mary Magdalene – an outsider who was understood and loved by Jesus.
2. Elizabeth Barrett Browning – loved, lived, felt, wrote on a deep level.
3. Margaret Thatcher – lady who overcame major obstacles to pioneer leadership.
4. Georgia O'Keefe - talented artist who dared to paint and live outside the box.
5. Julia Child – elevated the art of cuisine in the kitchen.
6. Glynnis Peterson – dispenser of good cheer.
7. Mary Ann Kimball – teacher and example of stalwart traits.
8. Joan Kastner – outstanding listener, creative communicator, and precious friend.

Margaret Thatcher, Georgia O'Keefe, and Julia Child lived during my lifetime. I know them from written stories and watching them on television. Browning and Magdalene require more imagination since they lived many years ago. They are not of lesser importance, however. Glynnis Peterson and Mary Ann Kimball were part of my life's journey. Joan Kastner is a friend who lives many miles away. The influence of the last three women on the list cannot be measured. These women were not famous. These women were ordinary citizens who became extraordinary role models for me. One left this earth recently. **Her name is Glynnis.** She wore her long pure white hair in a neat French twist. She was ninety-one. Glynnis was the mother of nine children. She was a stay at home mom during the day. When her husband of sixty years plus came home from his work, Glynnis went to a local hospital to serve as a nurse during the evening hours. This plan provided food and clothing for the family. After the children had all married and established families of their own, Glynnis cared for her ailing husband for many years at Calvary Cooperative in Golden Valley. Wisely, Glynnis arranged for a relief from one of her daughters in the care taking process to get out of the apartment for a respite. She did not sit and bemoan her status. Glynnis was hired by McDonalds to be a hostess and greeter. She would circle among the diners pouring extra servings of coffee and chatting with each person as though they were guests in her own home. Every patron enjoyed seeing and conversing with her. David and I met Glynnis at McDonalds. We would stop in for a quick breakfast and have a few words with her. We often talked about Jesus. Glynnis always greeted us with her warm, genuine smile. As we walked out the door she would call out, "so glad you came. You made my day." She possessed the ability to listen intently yet perform her duties. She established a record for being the oldest employee of the company. She also had the longest work record.

In the last few years she could not walk the several blocks to McDonalds so she made arrangements for another resident of Calvary Cooperative to drive her to and from the restaurant.

Glynnis worked there until just a few weeks before she departed this life. My father lived in the same senior building. He told David and I that you could always count on a smile and positive comment from this dear lady. My observation is that she swished God's love, like sunshine, everywhere she went. Glynnis inspires me to try to do the same in my remaining days on earth.

Another woman who greatly influenced my life departed the earth in midsummer of the year 2005. **Her name is Mary Ann.** This unusual person lived many years alone. She survived by making friends of younger persons, mostly voice students she taught at MacPhail Music School, part of the University of Minnesota. Mary Ann was a deeply committed person. She studied the Bible on a regular basis. She tried to put into practice the guidelines it teaches. This meant regular visits to those living in retirement facilities. She made recordings of books for the blind. She often wrote little notes of encouragement. Mary Ann mailed them to distant, but not forgotten friends. Mary Ann loved great music and attended many concerts and operatic performances in the Twin Cities. She developed her own unique style of teaching, taking the best from a variety of schools of thought. She had a great sense of humor. I was one of her voice students. Mary Ann and I would often break out with huge bursts of deep laughter when she would give an example of breath techniques. She was always careful to praise successes and encourage progress without direct criticism of performance. When I became a stockbroker at Merrill Lynch she became one of my clients. She was an astute investor who studied and knew what she was doing. She asked thought provoking questions. Gradually through the years she and I became good friends. When David and I set up our own financial planning business she worked part time for us. We had many deep conversations during lunch. One of the many things I remember was her statement, "the more you recognize God at work in your life the more you will discover what He does." Mary Ann was also a positive person, like Glynnis. I never heard her gossip or speak any negative words. Daily I try to emulate her fortitude in dealing with the vicissitudes of life.

A woman who is still on this earth has also been a role model for me. **Her name is Joan.** I met Joan through Mary Ann. Joan is a war bride from England. My first memory of her is sitting at my desk in the Merrill Lynch office. She was extremely quiet. Her body posture was one of withdrawal. I could barely hear her speak. Joan is a spectacular example of the human potential. She is today an elegant, poised lady who can stand before a crowd and present ideas in clever, imaginative ways. She can keep her listeners on the edge of their seats. Joan moves with confident grace. Her wardrobe ensembles are artfully composed. A comment from our manager at Merrill Lynch gives a good summary. After hearing her speak for The United Way, he came to my office and said, "Joan is one classy lady." I agreed with him and still do. Joan always speaks words of encouragement. I never hear her proclaim negative thoughts. She surpasses any participants on television survivor shows. During her life experiences she met challenges face forward and dealt with them. Joan knew the terror of seeking bomb shelters as the Germans bombed London time and again. She knew the fear of leaving her homeland to live in a land with customs and attitudes strange to her. She took the risk of marrying an American soldier. Later in the relationship she discovered the dark side of this man who was no longer simply a war hero.

When I remember Joan I once again renew my belief that each human being CAN grow into the exact flower that the Creator designed them to be. My recollections of lunches and phone conversations with Joan always bring me encouragement. Joan has sharp focus and determination. She can take on a new project and make it sizzle with success. Each day I try to grow as Joan has done and is still doing.

* * * * *

How very thankful I am that my journey on this planet intersected the lives of these three delightful and unusual women. They helped me be a better person. I hope that I have been a role model for other women in my life. I pray daily to be an encouragement as I have been encouraged.

Medicine Then and Now
"something to think about"

"It is only by the grace of God that people survive the hospital experience." This is a quote from a friend who is a registered nurse with advanced degrees. Another friend with the same credentials advised me to avoid hospitals since they are very dangerous places. Can it be that the advanced degrees in nursing gave them special insight? They are not from a bygone era. They did not serve in the medical profession in the dark ages.

Doctors and nurses were revered in the days of my youth. They were the experts. We followed orders. So when I began having irregular heartbeats and weird sensations in my chest cavity I made a visit to our family doctor.

Finding no evidence of heart problems he sent me to a noted cardiologist in the city. Just in case I had a heart attack, he thought it wise to have a back up to his diagnosis. The cardiologist did his routine and came up with an astounding conclusion. His prescription was:
1. Learn and practice relaxation techniques. 2. See a counselor at the church for what was troubling me. This was a bit of a shock since I was not aware that anything was troubling me. Sure life had its moments but did not every person experience the same thing? Assuming the noted doctor knew something that I did not know I began a series of visits to a counselor. After a period of time, the counselor told me I was more normal than he was! There was one problem however, the irregular heartbeats and strange sensations continued. Not only did they become more severe and

frequent but also I now found myself confusing my clients at the financial firm.

A typical phone call at my office would sound something like this (deep breathing and panting) "Good morning, Mr. Hefflewiffle. (deep breathing and panting) I believe this is an excellent time to add to your portfolio. (deep breathing and panting)" Often there was complete silence at the other end of the phone. Finally I would hear the client exclaim, "It this some kind of joke?"

I could not stop this behavior. I tried holding the phone as far away from my face as possible hoping to muffle the breath portions. Finally, I dialed the world famous renowned Mayo Clinic. When I spoke to a doctor's assistant, I was told to report the very next day. This was not the normal procedure for the clinic. The protocol was a written referral from your physician followed by weeks of waiting. I never did learn whether the assistant thought that I was a complete nut case that needed to be kept from society, or that he thought my situation would be the discovery of a new ailment giving the Mayo Clinic another achievement for their global acclaim.

After a week of intense scrutiny, many tests, the lead physician told me that I would be given a small cup of a liquid to drink. I was to avoid food and water until the following morning. He said they were going to give me a Geiger counter test. Did they think I had ingested metals, gold or silver? I would have told them they were going too far except at this point I had great difficulty controlling my body movements. I squirmed in my chair. My feet would tap the floor. I could not stop the movements.

During the Geiger counter test I heard a loud and rapid tap, tap, when the gismo passed over my throat. Immediately after the test I was taken to the lead doctor's office again. "Your thyroid gland is extremely active," he said, "We did not detect this earlier because the thyroid is not enlarged. It is much too agitated to placate with medication. Your thyroid is so small that surgical removal is a dangerous proposition. Some of your vocal cords could be severed with permanent damage to your voice. Our best option is to give you a Molotov cocktail."

That afternoon I was ushered into a dimly lit anteroom by an attendant in a space like suit. He quickly departed. I saw an open door leading to an even darker room. I heard a voice that sounded like an echo in a long tunnel. "Come in, Oceola." There I faced a technician wearing a steel workers helmet. His body was enclosed in a padded lead lined suit. His hands were encased in the kind of gloves you see astronauts wear as they are boarding the space shuttle.

The strange echoing voice spoke to me again. "Oceola, come, take this cup. Drink the entire contents. Then you may leave." He was holding a long lance like pole in his gloved hands. At the end nearest me was a large cup with vapors swirling out of it. I thought of a witches brew in a Halloween movie. I began to drink from the cup. The liquid tasted bitter and putrid at the same time. It was difficult to drink such a large quantity."

As my husband and I were driving to home from the Mayo Clinic, I read out loud the instructions we were to follow. He was advised to keep as far as possible from me. He was told not to even use the same bathroom that I did for at least one week. Was this medicine in the dark ages?

One of our family keepsakes is an encyclopedia of nursing. It was given to my husband's mother when she completed her nurse's training at Philadelphia's Graduate Hospital. The year was 1925. It contained the most up to date data of that time. Curiously, we turned to the section on treatments for thyroid diseases. Here is what we read:

"The diet should be plentiful, an accurate account kept of the food ingested, and the caloric value figured accurately, because it is imperative that these cases be given 5,000 calories or more of food per day. The patient should be kept quiet. All depressing topics of conversation must be omitted. Anything which would arouse the excitement of the patient, such as dazzling headlines in the current newspapers, melodramatic stories, and trashy magazines, must not be permitted. Since the slamming of windows and doors always causes a sudden shock to the patient, great care should be taken to see that it is not done. In other words, the medium in which the patient lives must be calm, serene and peaceful."

Dear reader, you are intelligent and logical. I would like to pose an important question to you. Which treatment appears to be more like medicine from the dark ages? Eating 5000 calories per day in a tranquil setting or drinking a Molotov cocktail?

* * * * *

Sometimes it is fun to look at serious situations of the past with light hearted humor.

A Ricochet

"lesson from an unexpected place"

I held onto the rail as I descended. It was a
long curving grand staircase, like something you
might expect to see in a prestigious Southern mansion
along the Mississippi. At the foot of the staircase was
an imposing fireplace. To the left of it was a lovely
baby grand piano. It was with both fear and
excitement that I approached the daunting instrument.
It had been over five years since we sold the baby
grand piano in our home "up north". We were
preparing to downsize. It was a given that our new
home would not be large enough to house the piano
that had been in David's family since the second
World War.

My fingers felt stiff as I sat down on the piano
bench and opened the Methodist Hymnal. Quickly
leafing through the pages I searched for an easy start.
It had to be something with no sharps or flats. Oh, yes,
here was one I used to play after the evening farm
chores were done. Mom and Dad would sit on the
sofa to rest while I sat at the upright and rewarded
them for paying for my music lessons. The repertoire
consisted of hymns in those days. The three of us
would sing with harmony. The words of the old
familiar songs blessed us, each in our unique way. The
memories were sweet of those times. It was for that
reason I decided to have those gathered at Dad's
memorial service to sing one of his favorites.

"Jesus, keep me near the cross.
There a precious fountain,
Free to all, a healing stream
Flows from Calvary's mountain

Near the cross, near the cross
Be my glory ever.
Til I reach that peaceful shore,
Just beyond the river."

Now once again I was going to play hymns.
Would my playing have a good effect on the spirit of
those listening? Soon I found an easy hymn and with
heart pounding I fingered the notes. With each phrase
it became easier. Finishing the first song, I boldly
searched for another. Soon the once deserted hallways
were filled with men and women making their way
toward the sound of the music. They sat quietly down
and watched. One fragile lady whose head just cleared
the top of the piano came to my side. She started to
sing. I joined her. When we finished she said, "That
was wonderful. Play the song across the page. I don't
know that one and would like to learn it."

"That makes two of us," I responded. Gingerly
I played out the melody, yes, I remembered now how
to sight read. This was fun! When I finished the little
gray haired woman said, "Oh that was pretty."

"Were you a soloist?" I asked, "You sing well."
"Danka" she said. "That means thank you in
German," she added just in case I didn't get it. My
mother's father was German I told her.

Her soft blue eyes showed excitement. "I spoke
English in school but my parents insisted we speak
German in the home." "We did not like that as
children," she continued, "but it came in handy
during the great depression." "I was one of the few
ladies who found work and it was because I spoke
German."

"God knew you would need that skill, so He had your parents make sure you learned their native tongue." I said, knowing this was a risky remark to a stranger. But the Holy Spirit had guided me. She nodded her head in agreement.

"I am ninety years old," she announced.

"How wonderful," I said.

"Play some more songs," she commanded. And so I did, until David announced it was time to begin. We had been asked by Rev Diane Lawson to hold Sunday services while she vacationed up north with her family. My first thought had been, oh these people won't even know what we are saying. But how wrong! Each one followed along in the hymnals, offered many praise statements to God, and gave a few prayer requests. One was for a lady in the building who wasn't feeling well. Her name was Bell.

So Dave read verses from Isaiah about God comforting His people. I read some verses from Psalm 139 about God knowing even when we sit or stand. Eager faces took it all in.

After the short service we remained to talk with the folks who had gathered. No one left. Each was eager to tell his or her story. Some said they had no family left. Some said that God had watched over them and guided them to this safe place, no longer living alone.

During the exchanges of conversation I noticed that an attendant motioned for one of the ladies who used a walker to leave the room. She returned shortly and came to me. Bell died during the night in her sleep she said. Bell always sat at my table she said. Bell was the one we had prayed about.

"You will miss her," I said. "Yes," she murmured softly. "My request to God is that I be allowed to die in my sleep," I told her. The woman looked up at me with longing for comfort. "My husband and I were reading some of John Wesley's journal aloud to each other this week I told her. You know that John Wesley was the founder of Methodism."

She nodded her recognition. "He wrote a nice thought about our death, I continued. "He wrote that each of us are like flowers. We come into full bloom just before we leave the earth. As our petals fall off, God sends angels to carry them on the winds to our home in Heaven."

"That's beautiful," she said softly.

When we had entered the building earlier, we saw two squad cars parked at the front door. We knew a death or accident had occurred. The scene had prepared me to speak to the woman calmly.

We continued our conversations with the folks who had gathered. I shared with them that David and I met many years ago in church. That the first question he asked me was, "Are you one of the nurses?" I added that his mother was a nurse. The men quickly caught the idea and got a good chuckle. Each one held our hands warmly as we said goodbye.

We had visited with the family of God, the forgotten ones in society, but the lovely ones in God's eyes. He has crowned them with white hair, a sign of glory, according to Scripture. I thought of Jesus who appeared to John. His description included "his hair was pure white." Yes, God, is preparing these dear ones for a life with Jesus, the mighty God, Wonderful Counselor, King of Kings. God does not forget them. They are in full bloom, just waiting for their petals to drop.

Their presence blessed me. God had opened my blind eyes and crumpled my opinionated attitude. I asked His forgiveness for my thoughts about to His special flowers. As we drove home, I felt God had taught us a lesson not learned in church. Was that why Jesus, who attended the synagogue, spent so much time out and about? Mingling with His father's children?

Adventures on Lake Harriet
"crossroads"

It was the start of a Dream for two old boys. David's fascination with sailing began around age six while playing with his model wooden sailboat. He and his Dad would sail the boat at Tookany Creek near home. Chuck would watch the sails on the many lakes in the Twin Cities and dream of one day sailing his own boat. Chuck was recently retired. Chuck had just married a renowned Minneapolis pediatrician, Dr. Jean. David and I were recently retired. The four of us had time and financial resources to pursue the DREAM.

On a balmy summer evening the four of us met at the boathouse on the shores of Lake Harriet to take the first step. Each year the Minneapolis Park Board offers sailing lessons for the popular sport in the Land of Ten Thousand Lakes. As golden oldies we soon discovered the other class members consisted of twelve energetic 'yuppy-duppies' [My name for people aged 25 through 30]. The Yuppies looked us over and offered reserved but polite smiles.

The first lesson consisted of learning the terminology used in sailing. It is a foreign language designed to keep landlubbers ignorant of what is happening when they are guests on board a sailing vessel. It also serves to impress one's friends in conversation. In addition to being taught the language of sailing, we learned how to tie ropes in fancy knots. It should be duly noted that David and Chuck quickly grasped the knot tying technique. Dr. Jean and I fumbled pitifully. Of course ALL the 'yuppy duppies' easily mastered the various twists and loops.

Lesson two consisted of a swimming test. The theory behind this is that sailboats have a reputation of flipping over. This is especially true when manned by neophytes. Dr. Jean slid into the water gracefully. I followed. Chuck Reinhold the Third, boldly ran to the placid water at the shore, then smacked into the water like a snorting whale. David had never learned to swim as a youth. This was rather unusual considering his sailing aspirations. Early in our marriage he expressed his desire to sail around the world. The idea was not too appealing to me. I suggested he take swimming lessons as the first step. Arrangements were promptly made for a series of private lessons at the local sports and health club. The swim coach was amazed at the results of the lessons. David made all the right motions, but managed to swim backwards. The instructor commented that he had never encountered a student who could perform such a feat.

David finally mastered the art of swimming FORWARD while on his back. It was quite a sight that early evening in the presence of the yuppies to watch the tall gray bearded man plodding the water on his back, long legs and arms flapping like a frog. He passed the test.

Lesson number three was what we were all waiting for. It was a chance to actually get on board one of the Park Board's sailboats, to get the feel of the rocking of the vessel in the water. Our instructors paired off the group into sets of four. For some reason, they placed us four oldies into the same boat. Chuck eagerly stepped unto the boat. Dr. Jean hopped aboard deftly followed by David who easily made the transition with his long legs. I proceeded gingerly. As I placed one foot on the vessel it moved away from the dock. I now had one foot on the deck with the other foot precariously still on the dock. I screamed for help trying valiantly to keep my balance while performing a ballet split. The three other oldies were a little slow to react. Fortunately, a strong young instructor leaped to the rescue giving me a huge shove. I landed in the boat and promptly sat down. Things seemed to swirl about while my arms and legs shook. It took two weeks before I was able to walk without excruciating pain. It is significant to note, none of the 'yuppie-duppies' had problems boarding the park board's sailing vessels.

Chuck Reinhold the Third was not to be outdone by my little mishap. The very next week for lesson number four he leaped unto the sail boat, grabbed the mast, lost his balance, pulled the boat to a near flip, Chuck bathed the entire backside of his shorts in the lake. It was an interesting sight to see, this dignified elder statesman with his fanny in the water, his hands latched to the mast, and a look of total astonishment on his face. Dr. Jean, David and I could not suppress our laughter. The golden oldies were beginning to establish a reputation with the yuppies AND the Park Board instructors. But would the four quit now? Definitely not!

It was on lesson five that Dr. Jean made her move to truly enhance the saga of the golden oldies. The Park Board instructors sent the class out two to a vessel on maiden voyages on the lake. It was another beautiful summer evening. Everyone was excited to at last be on a sail boat and be in charge. One member of each twosome was to maneuver the sail rope. The other member was at the rudder. At the Malloy boat David was in charge of the steering. I fervently pulled and released the ropes governing the sail. We were about half way across the lake when suddenly another vessel swished by us. It was headed in the opposite direction. We were amazed to see that it was Chuck and Jean on the boat. Chuck was the rope person. Dr. Jean was steering with the rudder. A sudden major gust of wind caught the sail of their boat. The speed accelerated the little craft and it responded like a "souped" up roadster in a drag race. Chuck hung onto the sail rope tightly as the wind gathered velocity. Dr. Jean stayed the course. Indeed, Dr. Jean stayed the course right into the dock area. Their sailboat was going at such a speed that their boat literally leaped over two privately owned boats anchored at the docks. This spectacular feat sealed the reputation of the golden oldies as not only dummies but dangerous.

Did the four quit? Absolutely not! Dr. Jean's pride and dignity were slightly diminished. However she was all the more determined to master the skill of sailing. After all, the oldsters had experienced a flush of adrenalin while on that wild ride. They would never be the same. It was indeed a crossroad coming of age. They then purchased a sail boat in Naples, Florida. Mr. and Mrs. Charles Reinhold the Third signed up for additional lessons from the US Coast Guard. They are now joyfully exploring the inland water ways of the area. David and I decided to pursue other endeavors which did not include sailing.

* * * * *

Recently David and I have developed a relationship with a delightful couple at a local club of Toastmasters International. The young man is a native from Australia. His bride is from Arizona. She speaks six languages and has spent time in various countries around the world. Together they have built two catamarans. They spent this summer sailing about the Mediterranean Sea on one of the largest catamarans in the world. It was designed by a gentleman from London who owns a company that builds sailing vessels. They have shared their adventures with us as their "adopted" grandparents. We now have tasted the pride real grandparents experience when their progeny is successful. Fortunately, we do not use a smart phone. Our other friends are spared the show and tell of this relationship.

As I think about the adventure on Lake Harriet I know that David and I selected the right pathway for us. As landlubbers we have not lacked exciting experiences. We both believe that when people listen to an inner wisdom they find true happiness. During the many years we have spent together we understand a bit of what the prophet Isaiah meant as he wrote verse 21 of chapter 30.

Class of Old Dogs
"senior jet setters"

Some barked. *Woof! Woof!* A few growled. *Grrrrr!*
Others wagged their heads. A group of twenty had
invaded the University of West Florida computer lab!
A pair of trainers quickly discovered a scary fact.
They had engaged an unruly collection of
independent thinkers blessed with some profound
blank spaces in the brain.

Someone once made the comment that "*you
can never teach old dogs new tricks.*" The old dogs
desperately wanted to demonstrate to the trainers that
this current thinking was more myth than truth. The
trainers, a husband and wife team, were professional
photographers. They made arrangements with the
University of West Florida to bring the old dogs into
the computer lab for *two* hours each week for **eight**
weeks. The goal was to launch the oldies into the use
of Photoshop Elements. This computer software is
extremely dangerous. It demands agile thinking,
steady paw movements, as well as numerous and
lengthy practice.

At the first gathering, the old dogs were
eagerly *panting*. Some black Labradors slurped the
desk with their saliva. Their paws were quickly
tapping the keyboard and shuffling the mouse. The
poodles sat patiently waiting for the trainers to do all
the hoops for them. Golden Retrievers *howled* loudly
for attention. This noise obliterated the voice
commands from the trainers. Boston terriers wagged
their tails as they struggled to take notes. The notes
were unreadable when the terriers returned to their
kennels. This prohibited practice sessions since terriers

are often lacking in short term memory. Two of the terriers share the same kennel. No amount of *careful sniffing* could produce a replica of the class session.

During the week between training sessions the trainers devised a scheme to keep the old "bow wow's" together and coordinated. They began the session by coaching each dog in the procedure of downloading pictures into the software. Even the bloodhounds had difficulty in finding the pictures once they were entered. Photoshop Elements software had successfully hidden the files. The aged dogs clicked their mouse with their paws to no avail. The trainers had to bob from one computer to another to assist each dog. Pandemonium was the order of the day. There was a chorus of howls, and whining. One dog actually managed to *freeze* the computer he was using!

The third session ended with one of the trainers insisting that each dog have a Photoshop Elements in his or her kennel. Each animal was told to cavort with the naughty software during the week. The trainers believed the play and practice would ease the pain of learning new tricks.

There was a spirit of undaunted valor among the old dogs. Most of the dogs in the computer lab hoped they would indeed catch Photoshop Elements in their teeth and run well and steady with it. Could the theory "you can't teach old dogs new tricks, let alone new technology" be proven false?

Please note: This essay was sent to the instructors of the class at the University of Florida's Leisure Learning Society. The husband and wife teacher duo caught the spirit

and replied that Doggie Treats would be served at the very
next class!

Post Script: One member of the terrier duo
became a rehab specialist. That dog now takes old
photos and makes them bear the splendor of former
days. The old terrier has also discovered a sense of
satisfaction in taking photos of people with many
warts, lines, and various wear marks, then producing
a presentable resemblance for a keepsake. Moral?
With patience, practice, and the passage of time, old
dogs CAN learn new tricks.

Confession! I am a member of the terrier twosome.

Intruder!
"A frightening experience"

The sound of a car door closing aroused me
from a semi-sleep state. That was no cause for alarm.
We hear that often in the late evening, and having
checked it out learned that our neighbor who keeps
later hours was the source. So, I lazily turned to a
more comfortable position in our king size bed. I was
just about to slip into a deep rest when another similar
sound pushed me back into consciousness. I thought,
"Well, our next door neighbor must have been
entertaining." Several more muffled sounds followed.
By this time my husband was awake.

"Did you hear those sounds?" I asked. "Yes,"
was his half-asleep reply. I slipped out of bed and
went to the master bedroom throne room. The
window in that room allows us to see cars in our
neighbor's driveway. All was dark. There was no light
shining through the glass blocks in his bathroom area.
It appeared that he had retired for the night. The clock
in our bathroom indicated 10:30 PM.

"Well, it's not coming from Dale's place," I
announced to David as I re-entered the bedroom. I
saw the mound on the bed and must confess was a bit
annoyed that he seemed to be not in the least
disturbed or interested in the source of the sounds. At
this point I had heard another sound like the closing
of a car door.

I walked the length of our master bedroom to
the French doors overlooking our screened in patio
and the cul-de-sac on which our house sits. Surveying
the scene I saw in the light of the city streetlight all

cars normally parked in each driveway. All the houses were void of lit windows; most occupants were probably in bed asleep.

"Well it looks like our cul-de-sac neighbors are all tucked in for the night. All appears to be quiet," I reported to David. No response. Well, he certainly can drift back into sleep at the drop of a hat! I thought as I glanced over at the mound of blanket on his side of the bed. Through all this investigation I did not turn on any lights. My parents taught me while living on the farm, that one was much more secure if you were looking out the window of a dark house. Our house with its many windows is really quite light even on the darkest moonless night due to the streetlight in the cul-de-sac and the streetlight in the front of the house. Light filters in through our closed wooden blinds.

My ears hear yet another sound. I decided to check the front of the house so I left our bedroom and was making my way around the curved wall when the front door opened! My body became statue like. The fight syndrome rose from deep within. I heard myself shouting with a voice, even I did not recognize. "YOU GET OUT OF THIS HOUSE THIS INSTANT!"

A second later I heard a meek voice say, "It's me, Sweetie." David, having heard the repeating sounds had risen to check things out while I was in the throne room looking out that window. He had left the bed linens in a human form mound accidentally. All along, my reports had been given to the hapless linens. My husband had looked out the front window and saw a red pickup truck parked in the street. He had decided to go out the front door to check it out.

Finding nothing askew he came back into the house as I began walking along the curved wall to the foyer.

Realizing there was no imminent danger, my mind relaxed. The aging body was not so quick to respond. It was reeling with shock as well as relief. My breathing was like being in a tight straight jacket; my heart was racing as though I had just finished a Grandma's marathon. "Oh, I feel like I'm going to pass out." I gasped to David. He helped me to the nearest sofa where I repeated the words "Oh, Ah, Oh Dear," etc. It took about thirty minutes for my body, soul, and spirit to return to normal.

Lying once again in our comfy king size bed we both heard the sounds again. We concluded they were likely the results from some military testing at Eglin Air Force Base. That sufficed to allow us to resume our decent into deep slumber.

Next morning as we were sitting in our recliners, sipping breakfast coffee, I commented to David that it was a very good thing that we do not keep a revolver in the house. Upon hearing the door open I would have quickly slipped to the bedroom and quietly pulled out the weapon. We could have been featured in the local News Journal with this headline: confused elderly woman mistakes spouse for intruder.

For two days following the incident I was forced to speak with a tender throat and crackling hoarse voice. The God-given fight syndrome had forced my vocal cords to utter the words with such force that the human instrument gave its utmost sound. David commented that if he had actually been an intruder he would have hesitated before moving a step further. That voice sounded so threatening and fearless. It gave the impression that the person shouting was holding a dangerous weapon.

We never know what we will do automatically when facing a sudden crisis. But we CAN be sure that when the threat passes the body will shake and shudder. I would describe it as a volcanic eruption in Hawaii. I see the hot lava streaming down the sides. It takes time before the lava cools and solidifies. Considerable time has passed since the incident. When I recall walking by the rounded wall and hearing the door open. I still feel a twinge of terror in the pit of my stomach.

Chasing the Whistle
"the aged versus technology"

We both heard it but said nothing. It was a shrill sound. My first thought was "Oh, dear, here we are with two new, not cheap, hearing aids for David. Already they are whistling." I kept my lip zipped. "Perhaps the sound will subside. Did not the specialist tell David that the hearing aids are very sophisticated and keep adjusting to new environments?"

The sound, high pitched, was constant. In a few minutes I turned my swivel chair away from the computer to look at David's reaction. I noticed the antenna on the box sitting on the desk where his computer was located. Now I verbalized, "Do you think the antenna is causing your new hearing aids to squeal?"

"Maybe," he replied, "I'll go out into the hallway and see if that makes a difference." It did not.

Then I recalled that our laptop computer picks up the signals from the box almost over the entire house. I reminded Dave of this and suggested that we turn off the box so it would not be transmitting radio signals. We disconnected the router from the computer and power source. The sound continued unabated. Being a wee bit frustrated at this point I said to David, "I would like to take that router box out in the driveway and smash it."

"What good would that do?" he asked.

"I might feel better," I said.

Fearing I might carry out my wishes, David removed the router box from the room. The sound persisted, just as loudly.

"Try taking off your new hearing aids and removing the batteries," I suggested. David dutifully went to the bathroom to follow my suggestion. However, the shrill whistle was just as loud while he was in the bathroom!

I walked over to his desk and leaned toward the sound. It seemed the monitor screen was the source. So, I bent over unplugging the power source. The sound remained.

At that point David returned from the bathroom having dismantled the costly new hearing aids. Even in his natural state he could hear the shrill sound.

"Maybe it's the speakers," he suggested. We both began working on the process to unplug and disconnect both speakers. Of course, being older, we are just a bit clumsy. One speaker was knocked to the floor. When I picked it up it rattled. Do I need to write that this only added to my already rising stress level?

The sound persisted, just as strong.

"It has to be the computer," I moaned. "This thing is only a few months old. You can't depend on any equipment these days. Everything is just put together on an assembly line. No one has any pride of creation anymore."

Once more I bent over to unplug the computer. My lower back was becoming sore from all the bending and twisting. "That's all I need," I thought, "Several weeks of bed rest to nurse a bad back!"

The ear piercing sound continued. My inner frustrations exploded into anger. I banged the top of David's desk with my fist.

I must pause here to inform my readers that David works very efficiently when things about him are in utter chaos. There were the usual piles of paperwork on the sofa, on the floor, on top of the wastebasket, and of course on top of his desk. When my clenched fist hit the desk, I realized that the papers had a slight rounding in the center of the pile. I quickly shifted the various items including rubber bands, pencils, paper clips, and bits of envelopes saved for note taking. When I got to the bottom of the collection, I discovered to my amazement one hearing aid. This hearing aid was not part of the new costly duo. It was the lonely one remaining after its mate was lost. It squealed even louder now that it was released from the clutter.

I handed it to David with the instruction to "take care of this thing." He placed it into the palm of his hand and released the battery. Silence returned to the Winslow house. Both of us began the process of reconnecting the computer system, including the router box that almost met its demise.

* * * * *

That, my friends, is one saga of the aging process. The scene also clearly shows one of my many faults. I lack patience and fortitude. Ironically my frustration vented with the desk pounding, produced a clue to the solution. Does our Creator use even our short comings?

An interesting post script: About one year later the missing mate to the single hearing aid was found. When we were preparing to set up for a special dining occasion we pulled out the leaf of our table stored under the sofa in the office. We spotted a small object moving in tandem with the leaf. Yes, it was the mate to the one who produced the shrill in the saga called "chasing the whistle." We are not sure how the missing aid got there. David might have removed it to rest his ear placing it on the seat beside him. Being distracted with the many tasks taking place in our home office, he might have moved to his own desk leaving the aid to fall and remain hidden for over two years. Some of the details in daily living raise questions that are not easily answered.

You will no doubt be wondering why a single hearing aid from the old set of aids was on David's desk in the first place. I will simply say that having Scottish genes, David wants to make sure everything is used to the fullest extent. He would switch now and then to the old single hearing aid. Does this make sense? Not to most, but to my buddy it makes perfect sense!

Keeping Cool, Over Time
"patience pays"

Do you find it difficult to keep cool when people do things that annoy you?

The Smith family lived next door to us in Minneapolis. Harold was an attorney for one of the most prestigious law firms in the Twin Cities. Wife Trish was a homemaker. The couple had two teenage sons, Peter and Jonathan, who attended one of the best private schools in the Twin Cities. As you might imagine, the Smiths were a busy family. Being dog lovers they had a large German shepherd and a mutt of advanced years. In order to save precious time, the canines were allowed to take care of bathroom duties on the lawn just outside our bedroom window. The frigid Minnesota winters were a blessing in this situation. However, during the heat and humidity of summer we were faced with two options: keep our bedroom windows tightly closed or put on gas masks.

One afternoon, the youngest son knocked on our door. He announced that the family's lawn mower was not working. Could he borrow ours? Wanting to be good neighbors we said, "Of course. No problem." The next week the young man knocked on our door again, same request. After just the smallest hesitation, wanting to be kind, we agreed to let him use our lawn mower again. Week three was a repeat performance. The hesitation might have been a bit longer. Week four…care to take a guess on what happened? At this point we had a discussion with each other. We determined that we should be good neighbors and "keep our cool." Week five unfolded in a predictable way. At this point David told our neighbor to simply press the garage door button and get the lawn mower on his own. Week six…smooth, proceeded nicely. Week seven, however, produced an added twist. Our young neighbor knocked on the door and made this announcement, "Mr. Winslow, your lawn mower is out of gas and your gas can is empty. I have only done half of our lawn. Can you get some gas so I can finish?"

David is a patient man. He agreed to get in the car and drive to the gas station to replenish the gas can contents. Yes, he managed to "keep cool." We had another discussion about keeping cool and being good neighbors. The end of summer came. Lawn grasses stopped growing. David prepared our lawn mower for winter storage. It had not been easy to "keep cool" that summer.

Mid-September Jonathan, face ashen and somber, knocked on our door to inform us that his Mother was hospitalized after a serious accident. The Smith family loved to sail. They owned a large sailboat on the St. Croix River. Nearly every weekend the family would make the forty-minute drive to the Stillwater Marina. They would spend the night on the boat and during the day enjoy the delights of sailing up and down the scenic water way. Jonathan's mother, Trish, had gone into the water to retrieve a buoy that had fallen overboard. While she was in the river an unexpected strong gust of wind whipped the boat around. Her leg was caught in the running propeller. It was gashed severely in three places from hip to ankle. One laceration revealed the bone.

After several weeks in the hospital, Trish was brought home wearing a huge cast. She was unable to walk more than a few steps and was weak from surgeries. Her husband and sons carried Trish to their bedroom area on the second floor. The family did not arrange for a visiting nurse, a cleaning person, or a companion for Trish. She spent the entire day alone on the second floor. It was at this point we began to realize that Harold, the attorney, was not earning sufficient funds to handle private school tuitions, mortgage payments, sail boat payments, regular household expenses plus the extra money needed to feed and care for the canine members of the family.

This time we were not facing a lesson in simply "keeping cool," but one of loving your neighbor as yourself. I volunteered to prepare extra portions of our evening meal and provide them during Trish's recovery. Have you ever volunteered to do a noble deed without thinking about what it means? For us it meant ignoring the urge to eat out after long days at our corporate jobs. It meant coming home at the dinner hour, stuffing unfinished work projects in our brief cases for completion later that evening. It also meant purchasing extra food at the grocery giving us an appreciation of the costs of feeding more than two persons. Three months and ninety meals later Trish was finally able to hobble about the house and assume regular household duties.

The following summer, the Smith family managed to repair their own lawn mower so we no longer needed to keep our gas can ready with ample supply of fuel. Our relations with the Smith family returned to normal for the area in which we lived, Tyrol Hills. Normal means you do not fraternize with neighbors, you simply give them a friendly hello when your paths cross while going in and out of your home on errands. Actually the unwritten policy is a good one and supported in the Book of Proverbs.

One weekend David and I decided we wanted to renovate our master bedroom, the one that has constantly closed windows for odorous reasons. We began a task of wallpapering. This was a brand new adventure for a couple who had no clue about the do's and don'ts of this art. It took the entire weekend to complete. Our blinds and curtains were removed from the windows so the Smiths had full view of our activities. Sunday afternoon, Harold knocked on our door and announced that he had come over to "admire our work." This was a bit strange since neither the Smiths nor the Winslow's bothered to survey each other's projects. We graciously chatted about this being our first and somewhat clumsy attempt at this skill. He commented, "You will end up with a mighty fine room." As he turned to leave the room he reached down and picked up a scrap of wallpaper and without further comment went out the front door.

One week later, Trish knocked on our door. There she stood with a package wrapped in brown grocery paper. "Here, she said, I created this especially for your newly decorated bedroom." She had sent Harold over under a ruse to get a scrap of the wallpaper so she could match the color in an original painting she did for us. We were deeply moved. It was Trish's way of saying thank you for the ninety meals.

As the months and years passed along the invisible bond between the Smiths and the Winslows surfaced several times. One afternoon I was home alone and had to call 911. As the ambulance orderlies were carrying me out on a stretcher, Harold ran across the lawn and called to me, "Hang in there, Oceola." He also waited until David arrived home from work to inform him that I was taken to the hospital.

On my fiftieth birthday, I announced to my father and David that I was going to plan my own birthday party. As my first birthday party, it was a winner! We had 99 guests for a buffet dinner held at the Minneapolis Institute of Arts. One of my Merrill Lynch clients, from Germany, planned and prepared the menu and food at the Atrium Café where he served as chief chef. The Minneapolis Institute of Arts arranged for docents to conduct special tours of the museum. The guests were divided into groups of ten. Each docent had a preplanned itinerary showing items in the museum that related to birthday celebrations. The official photographer took pictures and graciously provided me with copies.

All of this provides me with wonderful memories of that particular birthday. However, the most precious piece of that event was the fact that Harold and Trish attended. You need to know that Trish had a severe phobia of heights. The Atrium Café in the Institute was located on a balcony that overlooked the exquisite entry to the building. It was several floors above the ground floor. This was a terrifying experience for Trish to even attempt. She announced to me that she had set her face to get to the balcony. The couple used the enclosed elevator. They sat at a table as far away as possible from the side of the restaurant that was open to the atrium below. Harold had to go through the buffet line to fill her plate. "I would not have missed this because it was Oceola's special celebration."

DEAR JOETTA –

Thank you for inviting us
To be a part of your day,
your friends, & your thoughts.

Harold & Irish

"And in the sweetness of friendship let
There be laughter, and sharing of pleasures.
For in the dew of little things The heart
finds its morning and is refreshed."

* * * * *

How did "keeping our cool over time" benefit
us? We were blessed as we tried to follow God's
command to love our neighbor as ourselves. We were
given glimpses of our neighbors that we would never
have known. We discovered two delightful people,
who seemed to be "Difficult People," but in reality,
"Gifts from God." These are the kinds of gifts we
would not choose on our own. In the ensuing days,
months and years we were to discover a great truth.
The command to love your neighbor is meant to
benefit US!

A Gift With No Price Tag
"value beyond measure"

How would you like to receive a beautifully wrapped gift that is empty inside? When we spend our time with another human being we are using a valuable and limited resource for both of us, **time.** These moments, minutes, hours can never be replaced. Think of **time** together as a priceless gift hidden inside a box. The box outside can be lovely, inviting. But what is inside? Is it empty? Is it filled merely with perfunctory actions? Or have we placed within the box of **time**...the priceless gift of listening?

Recently I was having lunch with a pretty well-groomed lady. The day was sunny and temperature mild. The food at the four star restaurant was superb. We commented on the expertise of the chef as we sipped robust coffee and savored each flavorful bite. During the conversation I had learned the myriad of details about this woman's experience at the auto repair shop. After listening to her experience I begin to share the story about the little boy next door who wanted to swim in our bathtub. In the middle of a sentence the lady cuts in with..."*Oh there is Doug Demander just two tables down the aisle from us. He's the CEO of Prestige Corporation you know.*" Was this person really listening to my story? I wondered if I was a boring conversationalist.

When we give the gift of listening we focus on the person. We look at them. Their facial expression is sending us messages. The movements of their body reveal something of their inner state...peaceful, agitated, sad, bored. When we truly listen our mind hears not only what they are saying but also the nuances of pitch, speed of speaking, tenor of sound. We should become part of the story they are telling. We should be aware of how they act in the telling of their experience. Listening is simply, plain hard work. It is a gift of genuine love.

Husband David and I decided to attend the midweek dinner at a local church in Florida. We both feel uneasy in groups of people, especially strangers. We fail miserably with small talk. So before we drove to the affair we both decided to be active listeners for any or all persons who happened to sit at our table. We discussed several open end questions that might be appropriate to use. We also declared to each other that every person at that dinner was truly valuable and had wonderful characteristics hidden or displayed.

A couple sat down next to us. They began eating. We noticed that they avoided eye contact with us and that most of the time they looked down at their plates. I mustered up all the inner courage I could. Speaking with a smile while inwardly trembling, I said looking at them both. *"Hello, I'm Oceola and this is my husband, David. And you are? Isn't this a delightful way to enjoy a good meal reasonably priced and make new friends?"* They looked at me as if I had lost my mind. I somehow managed to keep on with efforts to connect. *"Is this your first time here?"* *"No, we've been coming here for several months,"* the fellow responded rather gruffly.

"How did you learn about the church dinners?" I asked. I squeezed my knees hard to keep from shaking, the introvert within was trying to take control.

The woman looked up and told me friends at the camp where they work initially invited them to the church fellowship dinners. Then we asked about the camp. Finally, the couple started to relax. We spent the next hour truly listening, nodding, inserting encouraging phrases here and there. The more we listened the more enthusiastically they talked. They smiled. Soon we were laughing together about their experiences at the camp. As they were leaving they both shook our hands warmly and said, *"How good it was to meet you. We had a wonderful time."*

* * * * *

As we were driving home, Dave and I commented to each other that we were tired, but felt good. We had the satisfaction of surviving a group social situation with strangers. We had learned a useful way to function as introverts without retreating to the sidelines. More importantly we saw the results of truly listening. We realized that any good thing we do requires thought and preparation. We had found a priceless gift, that is difficult to give, that has no price tag.

Keep Your Wits
"Focus is important"

It is important to have all your mental facilities functioning when you do ordinary tasks. My husband is an evening person. He manages to assemble all his functions only after breakfast, and the reading of the paper. Before that time he can be dangerous. One morning he found that the bathroom tissue roll was down to the cardboard so my spouse decided to replace it. He fumbled about the cabinets, located a new roll, managed to remove the empty tube, insert the spool, and then with a flourish he placed it in the bathroom holder. Shortly thereafter, the still sleepy man bent to tear off several sheets. Much to his surprise the entire new roll along with the spool did a quick flip and landed into the open bowl of the throne. The paper roll became water logged instantly, but the spool managed to perfectly slide down into the crook of the mechanism. It was beyond retrieval. A professional plumber had to be summoned.

Later that week I was telling my neighbor about the unfortunate event. She declared that Harold, her husband was also an evening person. Often he did not come to full consciousness until an hour after arriving at his office. He was an attorney at a major law firm in the Twin Cities. My neighbor went on to tell me the results of her husband "not having his wits" about him one morning. It so happened that later that day Harold was having a business luncheon with a client. He made a visit to the men's room only to discover that he had pulled his shorts on backwards that morning.

It is easy to lose your wits when you allow your mind to focus on other things while you are doing a particular task. Letting your wits scatter can bring potentially disastrous consequences. Several years ago I was getting dressed for an interview. I was scheduled to fly from Pittsburgh to Chicago to meet with officials of the Marshall Field Department Store. Since Marshal Fields is the bastion of fashion and correctness, candidates for employment must present a savvy appearance. I selected a stylish suit, carefully chose the proper accessories. A final look in the mirror confirmed that I was indeed groomed for the occasion. Confidently I drove to the airport. Pulled out my boarding pass efficiently located in the outer pocket of my brief case, found my seat settled comfortably, and enjoyed my flight to Chicago. After arriving at the airport in Chicago, I located the area for boarding the limo to downtown. The fare was fifteen dollars one way. When I opened my purse I was horrified. In all my careful grooming I had neglected to transfer my wallet to the purse that enhanced my outfit. Having allowed my wits to scatter I found myself in a strange city without funds, no credit cards, and more importantly, without any identification. The important interview was only one hour away.

At this point I was forced to gather every single wit I could find. If I called the officials at Marshal Fields to confess my plight, I could forget the interview. Who would hire a person who could not remember to carry a wallet and the proper funds? There was not enough time to have money wired to me. My best option would be to place my situation at the mercy of the person at the airline ticket counter. When she heard my story, she had pity. She agreed to refund the money for the return trip to Pittsburgh,

AND also hold my reservation for the return flight late that day.

Funds in hand I now boarded the limousine for downtown Chicago. I would be able to make the interview in time. However, one major hurdle remained. The limo fare round trip was thirty dollars. Now I would be short funds to repurchase an airline ticket for the trip back to Pittsburgh. This time even all my wits focused like a laser beam could not solve the dilemma. I resorted to prayer. It was a desperate prayer. It was answered. The interviewing officials at Marshall Fields presented me with cash to reimburse my expenses for the interview. This was not the normal procedure. I now had more than sufficient funds to return home.

Often times we lose our wits when we are stressed. Our minds are racing about trying to recall all the important details that need to be attended. We had placed our home of thirty six years on the market. Our real estate agent had tried to teach us the power of staging the house for display. Now a call came announcing that an agent wanted to show our home in thirty minutes. We raced through the premises, turning on lights, straightening magazines, and general pickup. Breathlessly, we finally drove out of the garage. David suggested that we might as well relax and have lunch at the renowned Oak Grill downtown Minneapolis. That sounded like a good idea. However, as I was stepping out of the car door I realized that in the haste of preparing the house for best showing I had not kept my wits about me. I discovered that although I had a lovely blouse and jacket with an appropriate pin on the lapel, I had neglected to pull on a skirt over my black slip.

Fortunately, it was mid-day so David and I made a detour to the nearest store where I purchased an appropriate black skirt. We then focused our wits on the pleasure of a gourmet lunch.

* * * * *

It would be nice to report that David and I now manage to keep our wits about us at all times. We do not. Happily, we realize that losing one's wits can produce some interesting experiences to remember.

Kitchen Follies
"boo boos beset us"

Our 26th President, Teddy Roosevelt stated a truth when he said" <u>If you could kick the person in the pants responsible for most of your trouble, you wouldn't sit for a month.</u> I learned that lesson as a new bride trying to impress not only my husband but also, perhaps most of all, my in laws. My husband's parents had waited for ten years for their only child. Naturally David was the focus of their love and protection. His baby carriage had a wide strap across the front that read, *"Don't kiss me, you have germs."*

Most of us realize that children seldom choose a marriage partner that comes up to the standard parents have in mind. I wanted to do <u>everything</u> properly to prove to David's parents he had married a mighty fine woman. Mama Winslow called asking us to come for dinner one evening; of course I said, "We would be delighted." After enjoying fine comfort food, David announced that we had things to do and must be going. The moment we closed the car door to begin the drive to our house, he asked me if I would consider taking in a movie. I agreed. We were surprised and pleased to discover it was a double feature.

Around midnight we walked up the steps to our house. David turned the key and opened the front door. A plume of dark smoke with a pungent odor engulfed us.

"The chicken!" I screamed. I forgot the chicken that I had put on the stove to cook while we dined at Winslow Senior's home. We found the stewing pot with a pool of black liquid in the bottom. Even the bones had melted during the many hours on the burner.

I had wanted to impress David with a tender chicken stew. He was impressed but not in the way I had envisioned. He spent every evening for the next week working on the burned pot. The Winslow clan from bonnie Scotland does not discard a valuable pot just because it has experienced out of the ordinary stress. Finally with a triumphant smile on his face David presented me with the now spotless stainless steel pot. There was only one tiny little flaw, the bottom was warped from the heat. Every time we used it we were blessed with a symphony of taps as it rocked on the burner.

My folly had other ramifications. Our kitchen ceiling now needed a paint job due to the many hours of smoke ascending from the burning chicken. David mentioned this to his parents. Undaunted, Papa Winslow brought his step ladder to our apartment to work on the ceiling project. My tall husband stood on the ladder while carefully painting the edge of the ceiling that meets the wall. His Dad held the step ladder so it would not tip. Mama Winslow came that evening for moral support and a second opinion if needed. I was doing my part using a long handled roller. No person, in this quartet, had experience in the art of ceiling painting.

Wanting to demonstrate my prowess in all things, I quickly rolled on all the paint in my tray. As an independent woman, not a helpless wife, I held the now empty tray in one hand while reaching up to get the paint bucket from the step ladder shelf. In a split second I could feel the thick oil based paint dripping down my face and spreading all through my hair.

Mother Winslow grabbed a bath towel and began sopping the sticky white stuff crowning my head. She kept saying, "Oh My." Of course there was paint all over the floor. David Senior grabbed a kitchen towel, knelt on his knees swirling the mess around. "Get me some rags, Son" he said. We don't have any rags my husband responded. This was our first paint job. Why would you need rags? We had brushes and a roller. "Then get your underwear, those that have the most holes." His father boomed. Faithful Scots pinch their dimes and keep holy underwear.

The next morning my scalp still smarted from the turpentine used to clean my hair. I was <u>confident</u> however, that the previous night's folly would be known only by the quartet. After all, <u>David's</u> wife was a mighty fine woman ! ! !

* * * * *

As I look back at this episode fifty plus years later I am truly thankful that our apartment did not catch fire. The pot with the chicken was cooking on an open gas flame. Fortunately I had the flame at the lowest possible level in order to cook the chicken to fall off the bone tenderness.

I am also thankful that the turpentine DID remove the thick mass of oil based paint from my hair. I was able to fulfill with dignity, my position as a department store buyer the next morning. The best blessing of all was the fact that my scalp withstood the potent turpentine cleansing with no irreparable damage.

Mountains
"special places"

It captivates my soul, this spot from where you can see three states, Pennsylvania, West Virginia, and Ohio. It is called Jumonville. It is in the midst of fascinating historical places. Luminaries like President George Washington and General Lafayette fought battles in the mountain foothills. Jumonville is a Methodist Campground Facility. It holds memories, poignant ones, of climbing carefully over rocks along steep winding, well-worn narrow paths to get to the top. Why was it so exciting to slip out of toasty warm beds, pull on rugged shoes, slacks, and sweaters with the plan to ascend to the mountain top? Our flashlights that we carried lost much of their effectiveness in the heavy mountain mist of pre-dawn. My fellow campers and I were about fifteen years old. We had precious energy. I use the word precious because at age 86 most of the energy has vanished like the mountain mists at sunrise. In addition to our flashlights we carried blankets which would be folded to form a seat to use during the sunrise worship service.

When we reached the grassy dome at the foot of the cross we all sat and began to sing. We included "Jacob's ladder" as one of the selections. Of course it was sung in harmony and with a flute as accompaniment. After the quiet singing we would listen to one of the Methodist ministers who were serving as camp directors for the week. We heard the old, old story of Jesus and His Love symbolized by the cross around which we sat. No words were spoken by the young campers from the time we scrambled out of our bunk beds until we finished our decent back to the camp. Of course the silence encouraged the mystery most all of us felt. Somehow we were part of the Moses experience at Mount Sinai, or the Mount of Transfiguration episode. It was a coming apart from the daily routine. It was also a corporate effort of fellow campers. We felt a strange kind of reverence while watching the sunrise illuminate the vast valley below with its towns, lush trees, and gently rolling hills. It was seeing it from a distance like the astronauts viewing the earth today. It was a glimpse of how things must appear to The Creator, more of the whole without the distraction of the parts.

When I checked Jumonville's web page, I was reassured to see that the summer season is solidly booked. How great to know that memories are still being experienced by campers today. How wonderful to be able to drive to the foot of the cross in our aged state and relive those moments of being closer to Our Creator. I am thankful that the caretakers of the camp site constructed a road way that winds up the mountain to the very foot of the huge concrete cross. The enormous size of the cross plus night lighting enables people from over eighty miles away to clearly view it.

God always surprises. He never acts the way we expect. He always uses His own timetable. I have struggled for the past several years to more fully experience Him. But I have found only routine valleys in daily activities. Our Catholic brothers and sisters call this the times of dryness. The early desert fathers wrote about it. They were more focused than I have been in their search. Oh, yes, there are times I have had glimpses of God. Just last week while visiting two of our church members in the ICU units at Gulf Breeze Hospital, I saw Him in their faces. I felt Him in the room with us as we talked and prayed together. These two dear old men have experienced some of the nightmares of World War II skirmishes in their life journeys. They are near the time when angels will carry them to God.

I still felt sad that deep within my being God seemed so distant. I wondered what I had done to have awareness of His Spirit depart. Then this week He presented me with one of his unexpected delights. I was privileged to have a special dream. Most dreams we have are what Dr. Carl Jung calls "housekeeping dreams." They serve a purpose. They help our psyche maintain a healthy balance in the experiences of daily living. Special dreams occur rarely. Dr. Jung calls these illuminating dreams.

In the dream I had managed to get in unnoticed to a huge Catholic Conclave. It was a gathering of Cardinals, Bishops, Priests, and even Mother Superiors and even Nuns. They were meeting to discuss the many issues confronting the church in our day. I wanted to listen and observe this activity from the inside so in the dream I put on my best incognito appearance and sat among them. While listening I became aware of a young priest about thirty years old sitting next to me. You could not ignore His presence for mysteriously He exuded overwhelming kindness. I was captivated by it and felt a peace within the deepest part of my being. I sat there no longer listening to the discussions around me. I simply drank in the kindness.

Soon it was break time in the dream. Everyone departed to get some food. I wondered around checking out the facilities. In the process I stumbled upon a large group of lay people. They were all mentally retarded. They were all genuinely happy. They all loved each other and immediately reached out to sweep me into their arms. As I reluctantly became part of the group of all aged adults in their non-cleric garbs I was astounded to see the young priest who had sat beside me. He was the leader of this group. At our church we call them Rainbow Folks. These are people who have various stages of mental development. He loved them with abounding love. They knew it and loved each other and me the same way. I was fascinated with the entire scene. I knew somehow that this young priest was the most unusual person in the entire conclave.

Soon in the dream, it was time to reconvene. I went back to the main assembly to continue listening to the discussions of earthly problems. I was amazed and totally delighted that the young priest sat beside me. No words were spoken. This time I felt not only His extreme kindness but His totally consuming Love. I felt myself melting in the purest of Joy. Then I awoke.

* * * * * *

As I recall the dream I realize it was a gift from God. The young priest was a type of Jesus Christ. He was among the church officials but not given any recognition. He gathered the lowly people at the conclave, those who society considers challenged. He had loved them with Divine Love transforming them into loving delightful creatures who in turn reached out to strangers like me. He had graced me with His presence as I sat in the midst of the movers and shakers of the church. He had filled my thirsty Spirit once again with His Grace, His Love, and His Gentleness. The dream enabled me once again to think with fervor and delight about the words penned by King David so many years ago. Read them in Psalm 34, verse 8 in your own Bible.

Amen and Amen.

One Day in February
"a special call"

That afternoon David and I felt the hand of
God guiding us. We received a phone call informing
us that one of our neighbors needed us and was
requesting a visit. We had visited with this couple just
a few weeks ago. Eva was a bit unsteady on her feet
then, but she insisted on serving us tea. We had a
wonderful conversation in their home. I knew that
Eva had cancer and before we left them I requested
permission to offer a prayer. Getting a quick yes, I laid
my hand on her shoulder. David and Philippe and I
formed a circle around this dear lady. The Holy Spirit
prayed for her through me. (He does that when we get
out of the way.) She was so very appreciative and
thanked me profusely.

As we left to go to Philippe and Eva's home on
the day Philippe called, I felt led to pick up our well-
worn copy of the Tanakh, the Hebrew Bible. When we
entered the front door Philippe reached out to hug us
both. "This has happened so fast." he said, "Just last
week Eva and I went to the library and city hall," he
continued. A hospice nurse was there. I asked
permission to read some Psalms to Eva. Philippe was
so delighted. "Eva is Jewish," he told us. Neither of us
knew this!

We followed Philippe to the bedroom. I
walked to Eva's bedside and gently took her
hand. Her eyes were closed. Philippe said to Eva,
"Oceola is here." She opened her eyes and instantly
recognized me. Her face lit up with a smile. I told her I
was going to read some Psalms to her. She groaned
and smiled. As I read portions of Psalm 19 and 34 she

was hearing every word. She groaned again and smiled. When I finished I touched her hand and told her I loved her but that God loved her so much more. Her eyes closed in peace.

As we came back to the kitchen I told their youngest son, Alex, who lives in Washington DC, that I had read to his mother. I lifted up the Tanakh. He rocked slightly and shook his head in approval. "Torah" is a living thing", he said. "Yes, I agreed. See how worn this is. We keep it by our fire place and read it often." I replied.

"Do you belong to Temple Beth El?" Alex asked. "No", I replied, "But we have been there to take classes taught by Rabbi David Ostrich. We love Jewish people. They are our brothers and sisters."

As we left, Alex held my hand tightly and said "Shalom." David and I exchanged the greeting. I had a deep peace within. I know that Jesus was pleased at what had just happened. He loves Eva, "a daughter of Abraham," and so do we. What a privilege to be there in His place.

* * * * *

Sunday, the First Week of March, 2009:
(Post Script to the February experience)

The Holy Spirit had more to teach me. His guidance had not only been **correct** but the **timing** was perfect. The evening that I read the Psalms to my neighbor was the last opportunity I had of being in her presence. The next morning she was transferred from home hospice care to West Florida Hospital

Hospice. Lesson: We must not delay when prompted to do something that is good and kind for another.

Eva lived only a few more days. At the age of 69 Eva was lifted from this earth to spend Eternity with Her Creator. On the day of her departure she told her family that her time was ended. She told her doctor that she was ready for the journey.

Only God, of course, knows the minutest detail about each person He created. He alone is Judge, Rock, Redeemer, and Savior. Adonai has determined the length of our days. He leads each one along the pathway of life on earth. Adonai knew about Eva's escape from the Nazi regime in her native Hungary at the age of five. God gave Eva the gift of many languages, Hungarian, French, English, Hebrew, and German. Her French language enabled Eva to teach in Paris at the age of 28 where she met her husband, Philippe, who shared her life for forty years. Her command of Hebrew allowed her to conduct symposiums in Jerusalem, Israel. The excellent mastery of English opened the door for Eva to become adjunct faculty member at Antioch University. She taught comparative literatures and world religions as professor at Wells College in the United States. Eva Hutinet presented a paper entitled, "The Mystical Experience of Teresa of Avila as Revealed in the Interior Castle" during a session on Religion and the Arts at the regional meeting of the American Association of Religion-EIR in Buffalo, New York on April 4-5, 1997.

Her funeral was held at Temple Beth El. We attended services. It was the first time we experienced a memorial service of our Jewish brothers and sisters.

The Rabbi read portions of Ecclesiastes reminding us all that there is a time to be born and a time to die. He also read the last chapter of Proverbs describing God's idea of a wonderful woman. He read from the Jewish writings about the Teacher, the Student, and the Student's students. (Eva taught Torah, both in Sunday School at Temple Beth El and as Professor at Wells College in New York.) The Rabbi read Psalm 23 with the ending words, "and I shall dwell in the House of the Lord forever." Rabbi spoke of the joy that Eva now has in the Presence of God. I thought of the phrase in the New Testament which states that eye has not seen; ear has not heard; mind cannot understand what God has prepared for those who love Him and live according to His commandments.

Later, on the day of the funeral, Eva's husband called and invited us to attend a "gathering" at his home. The daylight hours were almost exhausted. Cars were parking along the street in front of the Hutinet's house on our circle. People were already gathered inside the house as we walked along the pathway to the front door, others were following us. We were coming together to support the family of Eva Therese Hutinet, as they mourned the loss of wife, mother, teacher, and friend. We felt honored by Philippe's invitation. What we did **not** know was that the gathering was Maariv, the evening prayer service on the day of a Jewish funeral. The Rabbi greeted us and one of the leaders at Temple Beth El passed out books for reciting Kaddish. In Judaism, ten people must be present for Kaddish to be said. They believe that God is present then in a special way.

Near the end of the evening prayer service the Rabbi asked those of us gathered to share a story about Eva with the family. Most of those gathered were from Temple Beth El. I listened and cherished those extra bits of information about Eva. Then I felt the Holy Spirit nudge me to be bold and speak as a Gentile among Jews. I told them about Eva encouraging the young students at our Music Study Club Competitions by speaking softly to them as she led each one to the performance room before the judges. I confessed that I had given Eva, just before her surgery, a prayer shawl that the ladies from our church had knitted. I explained that the women prayed for the unknown person who would receive it. I also told them God had guided me to pick up the Tanakh, the Hebrew Bible, as I hurried out the door to visit Eva and read to her, **not knowing** she was Jewish.

The words flowed from deep within me. They were from God. After the service ended, the Rabbi's wife quickly came to me and hugged me. Other women hugged me saying, "What beautiful words." The Rabbi invited David and I to attend service whenever we pleased. One of the Jewish men, a leader in Temple Beth El, came to me, shook my hand, and told me he had never heard a Gentile call the Tanakh, the **Hebrew Bible.** He asked me what translation we were using. It turned out to be the same one that Temple Beth El uses.

Once again, The Holy Spirit had guided my words. They simply flowed from somewhere inside. I have since realized that when we speak of the Old Testament to a Jew we are implying that they are using something old and outdated. That had never occurred to me before. We believe that God, Jesus, and the Holy Spirit never change. When our Jewish neighbors read in the Tanakh that God is their Redeemer, Rock, and Savior, we must be careful to remember that Jesus came as a Jewish rabbi. Jesus told us that before Abraham was, He Is. From eternity's perspective, Jesus had already died on the cross for the chosen people as well as the Gentiles. God is outside of time. The Holy Spirit confirmed to me that I obeyed properly, by the hugs and greeting from my Jewish brothers and sisters. Once more I felt that Jesus was smiling. Once more I was reminded that Jesus gave us a very precious gift…The Holy Spirit. We must cherish and honor the Holy Spirit.

An excerpt from my journal in March 2009

Dance
"unending"

Can you visualize the bubbling joy in the faces of toddlers when they stomp their little legs in a crazy fashion? Remember those old National Geographic specials on television in which the photographer zoomed in on native tribes dancing?

What holds the fascination of tourists as they watch folk dancing at festivals? Why do humans dance all over the world? Why do rock concerts attract so many people? Why do they act almost as if they were in a trance? Is it a subliminal gene?

Dancing spans generations. It has invaded the ice-skating sport in the Olympics. It has become a popular television series named "Dancing with the Stars." Dancing with just the legs in fast motion with perfect harmony in the line of performers has brought fame to Ireland. The form may vary greatly but all involve the movement of the body. It is usually partnered with rhythm.

My husband's heart rehab sessions have focused my mind on the need for exercise to maintain reasonable health. Is there any activity more boring than walking on a treadmill with your hands holding a stationery bar? It reminds me of gerbils in cages running in those medieval torture wheels. Do those little animals realize they are going nowhere? Of course the action keeps them fit to exist in their prison.

My inner person screams out in protest when I walk just to exercise. But oh, what a wonder to walk along a new city street or meander through a garden or venture into a wooded area. It is also a delight to be free to dance. Free to allow the body to move in syncopation with the soul, with the music.

Penn State University's required gym classes offered a nice variety. I chose *La Cross* and *Modern Dance*. La Cross games soon became a cross to bear since I am allergic to sports. But the dance, now that was a delight. It was the first time a gym class was anticipated. We were taught various body movements, allowed to dance and express our inner feelings in any manner we chose. My whole being responded and in those precious hours of class I discovered a rush of energy that runners describe as "a high."

Dancing is part of my heritage. It springs from the Native American genes from my maternal grandmother. It trickles down from my paternal grandfather who loved to square dance. Grandpa Lansdale could not drive but he managed to arrange for a driver to deliver him to the many local square dances in Southwestern Pennsylvania. His wife hated him for that. She accused him of womanizing. But I heard Grandpa declare many times to Grandma, "Come with me. Sit and watch." But she refused to go. Grandfather Lansdale would take his sisters at times. They did not dance but enjoyed from the sidelines. Grandpa danced into his eighties. I had the privilege of dancing with him at a local Grange square dance one summer between college semesters. I could not keep up with him. He never seemed to tire. Later I understood. For when I dance the adrenalin flows freely. I am filled with a roaring sense of exhilaration. My love of the "dance" became known to my mother's sister, Aunt Muriel. One day I went to my dormitory mailbox at the University and was surprised to find an envelope from Aunt Muriel. This was the first and only time she sent anything to me. The envelope had no note, just a tract inside describing the evils of dancing. She was concerned that I would lose my soul in sin.

After reading the tract I was amused. I could not manage to feel guilty about dancing. I continued to dance in the gym class. I also joined in the dancing at fraternities. Not long ago a sorority sister found a picture of one of the fraternity dances and thoughtfully mailed it to me. The partner dancing in my life ended when I married a young boy with ancestry from Scotland and Ireland. He had never engaged in sinful dancing. His parents shared the beliefs printed on the tract sent by Aunt Muriel. I asked my husband to take dancing lessons. He said he would learn to dance when we were senior citizens. At age twenty-four you somehow believe that will never happen.

Although dancing with a partner was set aside, the joy was never forgotten. The dance gene within me remained and manifested itself in new ways.

Part II

Early in our marriage we spent most of our energy trying to excel in the corporate world. At five in the morning the sound of the alarm on the electric clock would pierce the soundness of our sleep. In a semi daze we would stagger to our feet.

Our first home was a house converted to a duplex. We lived on the main floor and rented the second. The house was a typical Philadelphia row house: long and narrow with no windows on either side. Our only bedroom was sandwiched between the living room and the kitchen. To get to the bathroom you walked through the kitchen to a shed attached like a lean to the back of the house. The floor of the bathroom was slanted downhill a good four inches. Often you got the sensation, after just waking, that you were on a ship. To offset this minor handicap, we purchased an automatic coffee maker. It was prepped the night before so that as we plodded to the bathroom through the kitchen for the *get ready for work* ritual, the aroma of strong freshly brewed coffee caressed us. It was indeed the one comfort of each early rising.

After breakfast we would walk several blocks to the elevated trains for a thirty-minute ride to downtown Philadelphia. Both of us were usually the first to arrive at our place of employment. Somehow we believed this would promote our careers onward and upward. After a ten to eleven hour day we would contact each other by phone and plan a rendezvous at the broad and market subway station. Sometimes we would stop for an Italian dinner at a family run bistro located underground at the subway station. Other times we would pick up a half dozen hot sticky buns at the end of our journey home. Those little pleasures were snatched up in desperation as a salve for our tired bodies. The dance desire for me became buried deeper than a grave-site with in my spirit.

In our free time on weekends we worked on projects, like steaming off layers of wallpaper in the duplex next door that had been purchased as an investment. We **did** learn to do a nice variety of tasks.

We re-pointed brick walls, filled concrete cracks in sidewalks, laid down tiles, cleaned filthy ovens and toilets after a tenant would vacate. But we were making progress in the onward and upward trail. We paid off both mortgages on the two duplexes and purchased a four-plex several blocks to the east. This gave us more opportunities to fill the spare time left over from our ten hours of devotion to our careers.

Sunday was our only day of rest. We would travel to center city Philadelphia with Dave's parents to hear the famous Dr. Donald Grey Barnhouse give superb lectures on Scripture. After the services we would usually have a Sunday dinner at one of the many fine restaurants in the area. Highlights of those Sundays were the times we traveled north of the city to the spectacular beauty of Bucks County. There were numerous country inns that made sumptuous feasts for Sunday church folk. Always on the menu one could find scrapple, a local breakfast food made of meat scraps, cooked wheat resembling Southern grits and laced with a variety of spices. It was almost impossible to duplicate the spice mixture so the locals simply purchased their scrapple from the area farmers.

Occasionally, on Sunday, we would take a trip to New Hope, an artist colony along the banks of the Delaware River that separates Pennsylvania and New Jersey. We would stroll along the banks and savor the relics of a once busy canal. We discovered a two hundred year old stone house with its own water wheel for grinding grain, and a dock on the river. The walls were two feet thick stone that was weathered gray. It was for sale. We toured the interior which reminded us of Century Inn at Scenery Hill where we held our wedding dinner. The layout included a living room, parlor, center-hall with elegant stairway to the second floor. A large kitchen spanned the entire length of the rear of the old house. The thought of owning and restoring this grand piece of real estate thrilled us. Perhaps this would make all our hard work worthwhile. Our grandiose dream was quickly squashed however, when we learned the asking price was $30,000. Even with our real estate empire of three apartment buildings we could not afford to purchase and renovate this lovely spot.

And so we continued our daily routine of long work hours laced with more work projects on our properties for four years. Finally the dance gene within me began to stir. I knew _true_ dance with David was out of the question. He would never permit me to attend dance classes. That would, after all, not be a suitable pursuit for a devoted wife. Those facts did not stifle the dance gene. It surfaced! So using some creative imagination I planted a seed thought in David's mind. In the seed was the desire for adventure. A book borrowed from the library called "Travel to Europe on a Freighter" provided the soil for development. I began reading portions of it to David. It was not long until the two of us were hooked.

We spent one year researching the places in Europe we had wanted to visit while still in college. Letters were sent to several shipping companies regarding passenger accommodations on their commercial vessels. The situation grew very serious when we received permission to go on board one of the ocean freighters while it was unloading cargo at the Philadelphia port. The chain of hesitation was broken the moment we stepped onto the deck. The dance gene exploded into a new kind of dance.

David and I would dance our way around ancient cities, country roads, castles, cobble stoned villages, tiny family run pensions and magnificent museums. We quit our corporate jobs and notified our parents of our plans. They were astonished. My Dad and David's father made the comment that we would be hurrying back to the States in less than a month. Our bosses thought we were crazy as did our friends. One owner of a manufacturing business that I knew through my work at Wanamaker's caught the spirit. He enthusiastically endorsed our adventure. We found a bottle of champagne and a bouquet of roses in our stateroom aboard the freighter. Joey Friedman had re-enforced his words of encouragement with action.

The sun was setting with a rosy glow as our one year old Norwegian freighter, christened the Havjeld slipped majestically out of the port of New York. The statue of Liberty looked tall and regal in dark silhouette against the sky. As we stood on deck watching the scene surrounding us, neither said a word. The carefully planned dance had begun at last.

Part III

The robin still sings vividly in my memory as I recall the balmy May evening in California, Pennsylvania. The little bird had flown to the sill and landed at the open window in the Presbyterian Church. Was the little creature attracted by the vibrations produced by the organ pipes? Or, was he sent by God? Some of our wedding guests believed the latter. They told us at the reception that it was a good omen of things to come.

Rev Benson, the Methodist minister of my childhood church presided at our wedding ceremony. There was a kneeling bench placed just in front of the pulpit. We had requested communion after the vows. We wanted our first joint action to be kneeling before the Savior and together receiving His Holy Communion. The Presbyterian minister washed his hands of any participation in the wedding. There is a law in that particular denomination that states communion cannot be offered to a particular person without offering it to all those in the sanctuary.

Since many of our guests were Catholic, we did not want to offend them. They were not permitted to receive communion in a Protestant church. As I write this, I wonder what our Creator thought of all these hoops and loops. Did He not declare through the writings of Isaiah His wonderful invitation "Come, all who are thirsty and weary, Come to me and be refreshed." The organ played the tune while one of our soloists sang, "Oh Sacred Head, Now Wounded." Even after the passing of nearly sixty years David and I are touched in our spirits when we sing or hear that precious hymn of the church. In a sense that time was our first dance together.

What is at the heart of dance? Is it to show off a skill? Is it a response to some primeval trait? In partner dancing is it simply an excuse to make *legal* physical contact? Trying to answer these questions bring to mind one of my many dancing experiences with the bearded Scottish man who is my partner.

David and I had joined several other couples on a New Year's Eve celebration at one of the country clubs in Minneapolis. We had had a white linen tablecloth type of dinner, with numerous courses. Stories were exchanged, laughter and friendly banter bounced back and forth across the large table. As black-tie waiters cleared the dining tables, the orchestra assembled, the leader held up his baton, and the music commenced.

Now I must confess that to this very day when I hear music I want to dance regardless of place or time or circumstance. I am envious of people who have the freedom to jump up from their pews and dance, praising God, down the aisles. I witnessed such an occasion in Vermont not long ago. One former priest, Francis McNutt (who wrote the now classic book on Healing), and the retired Father Gerzone (who wrote the popular Joshua book) led the procession. We were in the presence of Catholics, proper Episcopalians, and even some Methodists (Heaven forbid). It was all in good taste socially speaking, and I believe an event that delighted the heart of Jesus. Did Jesus dance at the wedding when He provided superb wine for the embarrassed host?

As the orchestra at the Minneapolis country club played marvelous big band tunes, my toes wiggled underneath the white linen tablecloth. So it was with delight when I saw Roger, one of David's friends get up from the table, lean over to the Scot, and ask permission to dance with his wife. I held my breath for the answer. David lowered his head and nodded his consent. Roger was a good dancer. He taught pro golf at the country club and traveled in those circles where dancing was a regular pastime. We whirled about the floor. I enjoyed every minute of it. It was a kind gesture on Roger's part. He knew that David did not dance. He was simply offering me the opportunity to enjoy this heady twirling and swaying to the rhythm produced by the chorus of instruments.

After returning to the table, I noticed an unhappy expression on David's face. "I'm going to learn to dance," he muttered between his teeth. This statement was exciting to me. At last my yearning was beginning to come true. Perhaps now I would have the opportunity to attend ballroom dances and flow effortlessly about the floor with my dear buddy. My hopes were dashed within one week. David was not the least bit interested in dancing. So the dancing gene was stuffed deep inside once again.

Years passed by. David and I became eligible to join AARP. Each of our personal physicians told us we needed regular exercise. So we began a daily routine of walking in our neighborhood known as Tyrol Hills. Every morning before we got ready for work we were out doors strolling along with our intricately carved walking sticks from India which we had picked up on a trip to London. We soon discovered the walking sticks had much more value than their elegant appearance. One could use the stick to point out points of interest. You could lean on the stick with each step when going up a steep hill. This action not only gave your body a push but strengthened arm muscles as well. They were also useful in fending off the occasional barking dog when it managed to free itself from its master's leach. It should come as no surprise to you that The Winslow's became the topic of conversation in the neighborhood. We were known as the mature couple with canes.

The morning jaunts were wonderful in spring, summer, and fall. Winters in Minnesota, however, like summers in Florida are ferocious. During January and February, wind sweeps in from the plains of the Dakotas, snow crunches under your boots, and the hairs in your nose become white with frost. All but the most hardy walkers retreat to area malls in order to continue the walking routine. We went to the nearest mall. We did not take our walking sticks. After the first several weeks the mall walking became boring.

If you know what you want, if you are patient, your chance will unexpectedly appear. One weekend I saw an announcement in the Golden Valley Community Newsletter that the famous dance instructor of the Twin Cities, Dean Constantine, would be giving beginner's lessons at the Golden Valley Country Club.

We often believe people will forget the statements we casually make. That is generally true, IF the person hearing your voice has the topic at the bottom of his or her priority list. My dance gene would NEVER allow David's statement at the age of 24 to become buried in oblivion. David's hastily stated promise to learn to dance when we were senior citizens bumped into a trio of other forces and connected. We WERE now members of AARP. Doctors had advised strongly that we exercise. Walking the malls was a chore. The Country Club where the dance master was holding beginner classes was less than a five-minute drive from our home. I boldly proposed to David that we sign up while reminding him of his promise given to me decades ago. He agreed. Perhaps it was the memory of the New Year's Evening dance with Roger at the Country

Club that prompted consent. Who cares? I was delighted.

Being age fifty-seven and age sixty, we were immediately the elders of the class. For the greater part of the first lesson the couples were taught the strict rules of dancing positions. Arms and elbows are elevated. The lady's right hand rests in the palm of the gentleman's left hand. His right hand is positioned firmly at the lady's left waist. It is the push and pull of these two contacts that guide the couple into perfect maneuvers. We mastered the positions easily. Then Mr. Constantine turned on the record player, reached for his assistant teacher and dancing partner. They demonstrated the foxtrot. That looked easy until Dean said, "Now let's see the class do the fox trot." Couples bobbled about. Some stepped on each other's toes. Others sashayed across the floor arms moving up and down as though they were priming a pump. "No, No." Dean called out. Remember the proper dance position. Your bodies remain poised in the position, only your feet move to the music. David and I were superb in keeping the correct dance position. It was our feet that were unmanageable. When the music indicated the beat, our feet did not move. When we finally stepped forward or backward it was with flat-footed stomps totally unrelated to the rhythm. I quickly adopted the unforgivable role of leading. Don't ever try to lead a Scotsman who is tall, has size 11 ½ shoes, and is very independent! We were in deep trouble. Dean Constantine and his assistant quickly separated us, Dean danced with me and his assistant danced with David. The elders needed dancing tutors.

My buddy of sixty years is not one to give up easily. He has marvelous staying power. We signed up for a repeat of the beginner's class. Dean Constantine commented that he was glad to see that we had not given up. For another eight weeks we stomped through the fox trot, the waltz, polka, and the swing mastering none. We had frequent tutoring sessions with no results. Once again we failed the class.

I was totally amazed when David suggested we try for the third beginner's class. When Dean Constantine saw us arrive he commented with a grin, "I can tell you kids did not meet on a dance floor." Inwardly, he most likely grimaced. Outwardly he kept his suave composure. Of course our fellow classmates had no idea that we had failed two previous dance sessions. Once again the bobbling of the beginners started with the first attempt at the fox trot. Strangely, the Winslow's feet moved at a reasonable cadence. Dean and his assistant focused their attention on other struggling couples. David and I were beginning to click. We passed the session. It was David who suggested that we try for the intermediate class. We were now able to keep up with the class. We swirled about the floor and at the end of the eight-week period passed the intermediate level class.

On the way home I asked David if he was game to attempt the advanced class. "Why not?" he replied. We passed that class with flying colors. We were now ready for the supreme test. On Saturday evening we drove to the renowned Medina Ballroom to practice our skills. After a few nervous attempts, we were soon moving about the huge dance floor with hundreds of other couples. I was lightheaded with delight. Several weeks later we were in the center of the ballroom doing the swing. As David expertly guided me in a twirl he said, "Aren't we something?" "I'll say," was my response. On some weekends David's good friend from Equifax Company joined us with his wife Gloria. Both were long time dancers. Other weekends we saw one of my brokerage firm clients dancing along to the big band sound with the live orchestra music.

About three months into our dancing career, I began to have frequent irregular heart rhythms. I became short of breath easily after doing the swing. Reluctantly, I had to admit my physical dancing days had ended as unexpectedly as they came. A recent quote from the obituary of Kenneth Richard Baugh from Pensacola sums up this time of our lives. "If you get the chance to sit it out or dance, I hope you dance."

Dance with the Divine

The dance gene stirs within me. It will not rest.
Rhythm fans the flame. There is no partner.
None to share the challenge, I am alone.
The music, the singers beckon. My shoes get kicked
off.
My feet feel the softness of the carpet.
My body is given freedom.
Lips and vocal cords mimic what the ears hear.
Joy is released within.
My singing flows with the body.
Energy surrounds me.
Tears run down my cheeks. I am dancing to God.
No other person, just the Creator and me.
Tears continue to overflow my eyes with complete
happiness.
In the singing my spirit utters, O God, I love you.
Suddenly the tape comes to the end.
No rhythm, no sound, still delight.
It was the end of an epiphany.
For the moment my dance gene was at peace.

Reality of the mundane returned.
Memory of that glorious time lasted.
That experience could not be repeated.
It was something to cherish.
My husband returned from his meeting.
Lunch was prepared, weekend chores fulfilled.
The epiphany could not be shared.
It was a special moment with Christ.
Years ensued, the memory faded a bit.
The dance gene is still within.
It cannot be denied.

Then one night in a dream a young man appears.
He sits beside me. Immediately I sense his strength.
He radiates love so powerfully.
I am aware of if without a word.
He gently takes my hand.
We move to the dance floor.
I am totally and completely happy.

I awaken in a delighted state.
Abundant joy touches my soul.
Another epiphany!
Even the thought of the dream
bring happy tears to the edges.

Time and the aging process
joined forces to negate the dance.
Mysteriously the gene remains.
Now I hear a voice not audible.
The source speaks to my spirit.
It says come. Follow me.
The steps will be both easy and difficult.
Take my hand.
Learn to respond to my pushes and pulls.
Focus your eyes on mine.
Eventually you will share my intentions.
Listen to the sounds.
The stars have names and sing.
Think only about me. We will become one.
When I give the signal, leap into the unknown.
Hold your body of faith firm.
Your hands stretched to mine of love.
Be assured I will catch you.
The dance gene I placed within you,
connects us. We will be one forever.

Dear Reader,

I was privileged to know many people on a deeper level than simply "Hello, how are you today?" Awareness of the treasure in others began when I listened to my parents speak to each other, thinking their little four-year-old daughter would not understand what they were saying. Sometimes they would spell a word to make sure it was in code. I learned words are far more than simply symbols on a page.

As parents, they did not realize that there is a silent language that even a baby can understand. As an only child I was free to learn how to read people's lips, to observe how they looked at me or other people. As an introvert I was content to be seen and not heard. That fact was a valuable asset. It helped me develop deeper listening skills. As a farmer's daughter I learned that even animals communicate with body signals. Every one of our fifty dairy cows had a distinct personality and responded well when that fact was honored.

YOU possess gifts, talents, emotions, wisdom and experiences that are truly yours alone. It is my hope that as you read the true episodes shared in this book, you were inspired to review your own life. It is my hope that you found stones and rocks of truth. It is my hope you discovered new joy and wisdom. It is my hope you will share, in your own way, with others. It is my hope and prayer that you will discover the Source of Life to whom this book is dedicated.

Yours truly,
Joetta Winslow

P.S. I used a pseudo name to avoid focus on the author.

Joetta

Mc Caig

Psalm 149

About The Author

Oceola Winslow is a pseudonym. Imagine the author, as your grandparent, confessing humorous, painful, sometimes embarrassing, yet true episodes from life experiences.

Through over eighty years of living, Oceola discovered rocks and stones of wisdom. The stones are sturdy enough to support walks at any age. The rocks can be used to erect pillars of truth that a person can embrace during inevitable crises and storms.

The author's roots are a small river town in the United States of America. Osceola's life has been molded by degrees in two well-known universities, realities of long careers in the corporate world, living in city centers as well as first-hand farm experience.

Winslow has been honored by awards from small and worldwide organizations. Life includes nearly sixty years with a spouse who is also a precious best friend.

Oceola considers any personal achievements like ashes that will quickly disappear with the sweep of a broom or a sudden strong gust of wind. The rocks and stones uncovered were in existence long before Oceola was born. The avid or casual reader of Holy Scripture will find rocks and stones used in many ways. Rocks and stones will remain for many years after Oceola's body becomes ashes and the spirit has returned to the Source.

Made in the USA
Middletown, DE
21 November 2018